The Radical Bishop & Gay Consciousness

The Passion of Mikhail Itkin

The Radical Bishop & Gay Consciousness

The Passion of Mikhail Itkin

Edited by
Mark A. Sullivan and Ian Young

With Contributions by
Mikhail F. Itkin
Rosamonde Miller
John P. Plummer
Michael E. Bacon

Autonomedia

For further information and/or to communicate with others interested in the subject matter of this book, feel free to contact:

Mark Aelred Sullivan
Circle of the Free Spirit / Liberal Gnostic Community
Box 230316 Ansonia Station
New York, NY 10023

Email: markaelredcfs@aol.com

NYSCA

This publication is made possible in part with public funds from the New York State Council on the Arts, a state agency.

Cover design by Gary Roscoe Johnson
Interior design by Jim Fleming

ISBN: 978-1-57027-274-5

Autonomedia ▼ Black Triangle Series

Autonomedia
POB 568 Williamsburgh Station
Brooklyn, NY 11211-0568 USA

info@autonomedia.org
www.autonomedia.org

CONTENTS

IMAGES FROM THE ITKIN FILE

"The moment we cease to hold
each other, the moment we break
faith with one another, the sea
engulfs us and the light
goes out." — James Baldwin,
as quoted by +Mikhail Itkin in
the second edition of *The Radical
Jesus and Gay Consciousness*

Introduction
The Itkin File

Mark Aelred Sullivan

Most Americans — Gay or non-Gay — consider themselves to be neither rich nor poor, neither success nor failure, neither privileged nor deprived. They have been carefully taught that they are simply part of the great middle and that, in a hungry world, they should count themselves lucky for it.

Our present time of crisis proves the falsity of that assumption!

We, at THE GAY ANARCHIST, don't count that as being a "lucky" condition to be in. Those arrogant with power have built a trap; and like lemmings marching to the sea, most people have fallen in. Those arrogant with power despise the *true individual* (the word means "one who is undivided in him/herself," in its origins), and so they try to keep us too satisfied to rebel, too insignificant to matter.

It's always necessary for the ruling class of the State to keep the people in a sleepwalking state. If they're hungry, quiet them with food stamps. Lull them to sleep with phoney promises of security, kill off the spirit of creativity by inculcating standards of propriety and conformity — keep a ritual scapegoat to blame when things go wrong. Calm the people... destroy the individual!

And now, as always in the history of the patriarchy, faggots and dykes are the ultimate scapegoat for the State.

But we have seen through this trap."
— Mikhail F. Itkin, CLC
The Gay Anarchist, Journal of the Libertarian-Socialist Gay Caucus,
May–June 1977, Volume 1, Number 1

"I am an Anarchist! Wherefore I will
Not rule, and also ruled I will not be!"
— John Henry Mackay, "Anarchy"

I. The Memory

"Karl Popper reminds us that... the losers may deserve more serious consideration than the winners.... the revelation given by Jesus was not otherworldly or mythological, but an uncompromising ethical demand that asked everything of those who followed." — Walter Wink, "Foreword," *The Lost Religion of Jesus: Simple Living and Nonviolence in Early Christianity* by Keith Akers, 2000, Lantern Books, p. xii.

It was the Summer of 1976. The Democratic Party convention was being held. Demonstrations were going on outside Madison Square Garden and Penn Station. There we were, gay and lesbian radicals — even anarchists (mostly of the non-violent peace-loving kind) — in the midst of the crowd. "No more shit! No more shit!" we chanted. Suddenly, about six or eight feet to my right, a short, round, black-clad figure spun around like a top then stopped and growled "Some of my best friends like shit!" It was Bishop Mikhail Francis Itkin. No doubt he wanted us to chant something else, and I believe we did. Itkin was known in the gay radical world as a non-violent anarchist and activist — as well as an independent openly-gay bishop. I marveled at the combination. He was a stumbling block to radicals and a scandal to Christians. He was born into a Jewish family and fated — or chosen by the Spirit — to be a stirrer-up of discontent, a "ring-leader" of anarchists, and, indeed, a great reconciler of the contending forces within society and, indeed, within his own soul.

On looking back, and rereading his scattered writings, it seems his practice of Christian love included embracing outcasts of all kinds, including those who like shit. He resembled his two patron saints: Archangel Michael who wields the sword of divine protection and vengeance, and Francis of Assisi who loved and consorted with the most lowly and suffered passionately for the love of Jesus. No two saints seem further apart. Somehow Bishop Michael Francis embodied them both.

Ian Young came upon the New York gay anarchist scene shortly after the Summer of '76, and we became friends. At that time, I had just launched *The Storm! A Journal for Free Spirits.* Ian and other gay and anarchist comrades were soon to contribute articles to the *The Storm!* and to other associated 'zines. Our local gay anarchist movement was growing. However, within a year Itkin left for California in what seemed like a divine huff. His open letters from that period were righteous letters of resignation from one or another political group he had been involved in. They were addressed to what looks like a who's who list of the gay movement at that time — it was a much smaller movement then. Apparently, he knew us all.

Bishop Itkin's writings from California indicated he would now renew his devotion to spiritual liberation as the basis of social liberation. When he left New York City, he left his 'zine, *The Gay Anarchist,* without an editor or organizer. A group of us, including Ian, started a group called Gay Anarchists, with its own little 'zine, more or less picking up where Itkin left off. The good bishop stayed in touch with me and with Ian for a year or so and then we lost contact.

Unbeknown to myself or Ian (now living in Canada), the fiery bishop had passed on in 1989. We found out years later and began discussing the possible publication of some of his writings. We sought out his remaining followers in search of permission to republish, but found that his heir apparent, Bishop Marcia Herndon had also passed on. We found no one who claimed intellectual property rights in Itkin's writings. We decided to go ahead with the idea of publishing Itkin's major work along with articles about him or inspired by him. The result is the volume you, dear reader, now hold in your hand.

II. The Works

> "The Spirit of Jesus and other prophets calls people to simple life styles in order that 'the people may live'." [95 Theses or of Faith for a Christianity for the Third Millenium, Thesis 35] — Matthew Fox, *A New Reformation!*, 2005, Wisdom University Press, p. 74

> "Bring me by bow of burning gold:
> Bring me my arrows of desire,
> Bring me my spear: O clouds unfold!
> Bring me my chariot of fire.
> I shall not cease from mental fight,
> Nor shall my sword sleep in my hand
> Till we have built Jerusalem..."
> — William Blake, *"Jerusalem"*

This volume is at best a first attempt to resurrect an all but forgotten figure — and his enduring significance. More research needs to be done. Indeed, we have not dealt with all of the material we have by Itkin, material I fondly call "The Itkin File." This material is a small collection of self-published pamphlets and "zines." They give evidence of Itkin's various attempts to start spiritual communities under one name or another. There is "The Community of the Love of Christ" — "an Ecumenical Religious Order for the spiritual renewal, consecration and transformation of Humanity through the restoration of the

Way of Living of the apostolic and primitive Church Catholic" proclaimed in a pamphlet dated Pentecost 1976. In this introduction, Itkin affirms the liberation message of the gospel today, "just as it spoke to the 'despised and rejected' of Jesus' own day," and decries the suppression of "the liberating Truth since 325 A. D." — long before the recent Gnostic revival brought it to the attention of millions of readers.

Ironically, for a radical, Itkin was concerned to affirm the validity of his efforts by an appeal to tradition. His introduction to the Community concludes: "(This Ecumenical Gay Christian Religious Order is canonically affiliated as a Province of THE SYRO-CHALDEAN EVANGELICAL CATHOLIC COMMUNION, sometimes called Nestorian.)" The address of the Community was 339 Lafayettte Street, New York City, the headquarters of the War Resisters League. Other radical groups, such as the left-wing Libertarian Book Club, were located at this address. The content of this introduction is a short version of the message of *The Radical Jesus and Gay Consciousness.* The project itself was clearly the bishop's attempt to put this message into practice.

A pamphlet dated 14 April 1977 shows that The Community of the Love of Christ had moved to 6326 Lexington Avenue in Hollywood, California. The pamphlet is addressed to a who's who list of gay and radical movement people and groups — all listed in alphabetical order (e.g. Industrial Workers of the World, Christopher Isherwood, Living Theatre Collective, Rev. Troy Perry, and New Yorkers like Ralph Hall, Flash Storm, Harold Pickett, Ian Young and myself). It was an open letter concerning Itkin's resignation from membership in the national Libertarian Party. He signs off as both the Episcopal Coordinator of the Community of the Love of Christ and the Pacific Coast Coordinator of the Libertarian-Socialist Gay Caucus. He had given up on possible cooperation with the propertarian Libertarian Party and affirmed his devotion to "the beautiful anarchist-androgynous community of sisterbrotherhood in Christ our Liberator: L'Chaim! L'Shalom! L'Cherut!"

An eight-page 'zine, *The Gay Anarchist,* came out, edited by Itkin, dated May–June 1977, as the journal of the Libertarian-

Socialist Gay Caucus, Volume 1, No. 1. In addition to following Jesus, Itkin was the follower of another carpenter, Edward Carpenter. "'To realize freedom!' That statement by Edward Carpenter sets forth the goal of this journal." Itkin goes on: "Like most of the world's population today, we Gay people are a colonized people. But there is one quality of our situation which is not shared by any other colonized people — excepting Women — and it is the condition which gives the Gay and Feminist struggle for liberation a very special role in the international revolutionary drama. We are the only colonized peoples who are born, raised and mis-educated right in the house of the oppressor. We are all people who have been raised in the patriarchal nuclear family, and only come to find our identity and our struggle as we grow." He goes on and identifies the goal of "the beautiful free creative community of sister/brotherhood, the androgynous anarchist society towards which we strive. Our goal, in the words of Jean Genet, mut be 'to pierce the shell of the world's contempt!'" Included also in the issue is a defense of the term "Libertarian" as originally meaning "Communitarian Anarchism" and a reference to Edward Carpenter and Michael Bakunin as Gay Anarchists, plus the Declaration of the Social Revolutionary Anarchist Federation. However, the gay bishop had not abandoned his Judaeo-Christian spirituality, and quotes Isaiah: "Awake and sing, you who dwell in dust... and the earth shall cast out its dead."

Coming in the mail to me around the same time, 1977, but undated, is a 4-page pamphlet on the "Order of the Divine Love." It was adorned by a Sufi-like winged Enneagram with an equilateral cross in the center. Itkin writes: "The Order of the Divine Love is an ecumenical Community for the Harmonious Development of Humanity and the Earth in Christ." The Order is dedicated to "the Sacramental Work of spiritual renewal, consecration and transformation through the restoration of the ancient Christ-Mysteries for the New Age." He harks back to "the Apostolic Community of the Pre-Nicene era" and links the Order to "the Aisor Historic Episcopate derived by the transmission from the Syro-Chaldean Evangelical

Catholic Community.... carried out through the agency of the FREE CHRISTIAN COMMUNITY." And he proclaims "Revelation did not cease with the Apostles nor will it cease with any age." Alas, for me, shortly after receiving this pamphlet, communications from Mikhail Itkin did in fact cease.

According to the Moorish Orthodox Church, Itkin's Evangelical Catholic Communion was "headquartered in Daly City, California, and had 15 parishes with 3,500 members in the United States and 6 foreign missions. Mar Mikhael (*sic*) was assisted by a Synod of Bishops...." (http://www.geocities.com/moorishorthodoxchurch/ITKIN.html) There is nothing in my own Itkin file that verifies this.

However, I was privileged to know and collaborate with the late Bishop Rafael "Rafi" Sharif, who had been consecrated a bishop in the 1960s by +Mikhail, for service in the Moorish Orthodox Church (from whence it got its designation of "Orthodox"). Rafi — with anarcho-socialist tendencies of his own (he was a member of the Industrial Workers of the World — the IWW or "Wobblies"), went on to found the "Moorish Order of the Resurrection + Greenfriars", in conjunction with the consecration of +Gregory Foster in 1996. Although the Order was never disbanded, it seems to have become dormant following Rafi's passing. Likewise, Itkin's heir, +Marcia Herndon, has also passed on, and it seems no one has taken up her ministry, although +Richard Stanuikynas, whom she consecrated to the episcopacy, remains an active bishop at large.

III. THE LEGACY

> Like Christianity itself, same-sexuality "turns the world upside down" (Acts 17:6) by challenging the so-called *natural* roles that in reality are *cultural*. Same-sex couples are thus capable of being truly natural symbols for the mutuality of equals, free from the traditional roles assigned by culture to men and women.... Further, as procreation is not an end for same-sex relationships, the relationship *itself*

> becomes the locus for its intrinsic goodness: that is, it is not dependent on a result that comes from the relationship, but on the relationship itself. Thus the partners do not serve as *means to an end*, but as *ends in themselves* — all being done for the good of the other, in mutual submission and love, in realization of the principle of "I-Thou."— Tobias Stanislas Haller, BSG, *Reasonable and Holy: Engaging Same-Sexuality*, 2009, Seabury Books, p. 55

> The Good News is that if Jesus could realize his identity with God, we can also — but this God can not be idolized as an imperious monarch with a royal court or ministering angels. God, as the "depth and ground of all being," the love which moves the sun and other stars, is something much more inward, intimate and mysterious — in the sense of being too close to be objectivised but always to remain the "Thou" of "I-Thou" dialogue, in community and inwardly, as Presence for us in Jesus our Brother. — Mikhail F. Itkin, CLC *The Radical Jesus and Gay Consciousness* (1972 edition)

Although there seems to be no direct organizational legacy currently in active existence, we can see that +Mikhail Itkin has given us in the 21st century a spiritual legacy. The independent sacramental movement is alive and well — and growing. Many are the heirs of lines of apostolic succession that passed through +Mikhail's hands. What we now call the GLBTQ movement has made many gains. Openly gay bishops now populate the Episcopal Church in America — a second generation to +Mikhail's first. Same-sex marriage is now becoming legal, as well as a sacrament (i.e., in the more liberal and progressive churches). Yet we still have something to learn from the radical bishop. Openly gay men and lesbians serving in the military is a mixed blessing — at least for those who take a religious or spiritual anti-war stance — as did +Mikhail. The gay and lesbian liberation movements that he passionately devoted himself to in the 1970s has to a certain extent become an assimilationist consumerist capitalist culture — no longer the counter-culture he hoped would flower. Have we in the GLBTQ community changed the larger society more than it has changed us to be like itself? Or have we succeeded in becoming — not liberated but — merely comfortable? Clearly +Mikhail Itkin would, if alive today, raise his voice to "afflict the comfortable" as well as "comfort the afflicted"!

Some readers today — particularly those most committed to rational dialogue across religious, philosophical and cultural traditions — might not be comforted by, or not comfortable with, Bishop Itkin's devotion to "Jesus our Brother". And while the editors did try to reduce repetition in the new edition presented here of *The Radical Jesus and Gay Consciousness*, most such references were retained because they reveal the inner life and ideal Beloved One of Michael Francis Itkin. To minimize this self-revelation — indeed, the very essence of the work — would be to consign *The Radical Jesus* to a curious academic event or theological exercise. Like all Lovers, +Mikhail waxes eloquently and repeatedly about his Beloved. It is well recognized that even when scholarly research is involved – surprisingly like spiritual devotion – one tends to find the Jesus one is looking for. For some, Jesus was a hard-core Jewish opponent of the Roman occupation; for others, a non-historical Pagan myth... One is reminded of the Gnostic insight that Truth comes into the world, or is encountered, through types and images (Gospel of Philip); and that the transcendent Light takes many forms and images, dependent on the receptive capacity — one might say the orientation — of the seeker. In the Apocryphon of John, for example, the transcendent Light appears to John in the "multiformed image" of a young boy, a servant, and an elder, and identifies itself as "the Father, Mother and Son" (the original gender-inclusive Trinity). And when Anthony Quinn, playing Saint Peter on the Hollywood silver screen, is fleeing martyrdom in Rome, he encounters a beautiful and mysterious young boy. Peter asks "Quo vadis" — where are you going? And the Boy says he is Jesus going to

Rome to be crucified again. And so Peter turns around and returns to Rome and his own crucifixion. Similarly, for +Mikhail Itkin, Jesus, the Divine Self, is experienced as his brother and his lover — as Love itself — and as One who inspires him to embrace if not physical martyrdom, the martyrdom of bearing witness to the suffering of others, speaking truth to power, and risking rejection if not much worse. At bottom, then, *The Radical Jesus* is a poetic and prophetic declaration — and an image — of Radical Love. For all of us, may this Image and this pioneering manifesto of gay liberation be a catalyst connecting us with our own Inner Beloved, our own Divine Twin, our own True Self — shining forth as our own capacity to work with others for our mutual joy and liberation.

Allow me to end with a personal note. It was on May 20, 1995, that this author was consecrated a bishop by +John Noel Murray and five other independent bishops, taking the episcopal name of Aelred, after Aelred of Rievaulx, the gay abbot-saint who wrote on spiritual friendship. As it turned out, among the bishops in my apostolic lineage was none other than +Mikhail Itkin. Life has a strange way of curving back on itself, like the Gnostic image of the Ourorobus, the serpent devouring its own tail — the Hermetic symbol of "One the All," of consciousness curving back on itself (self-knowledge), and perhaps of homoeroticism itself. Nietzsche's life-affirming myth of the Eternal Return is also made manifest here — living your life in such a way that you would be willing to live it repeatedly — again, again, and again, ad infinitum. One imagines +Mikhail Itkin would be willing to live his life many times over — as the sacred quest that indeed it was, with all its labyrinthian twists and turns. The self-searching for meaning and purpose in life provides its own fulfillment. Indeed, the radical bishop's life embodied the words of an old blessing:

"May you become the One that you are."

20 May 2012
Avatar Temple
The Bronx, New York City

"What *Is* an Itkin, Anyway?"

Notes on a Small Bishop with a Big Bishopric

Ian Young

> "Mikhail was a bit of a Holy Fool, tearing down a good deal of what he built as quickly as he built it; both ordaining and excommunicating people impetuously, being radical and vocal and outrageous. He was captivating, sometimes likeable, and energetic as only the manic-depressive can be. He was a tough little Jewish kid from the Bronx who made a remarkable journey through 20th century American religion." — Michael B. Music

The author of *The Radical Jesus and Gay Consciousness,* Christian anarcho-pacifist Mikhail Francis Augustine Itkin, was born Michael Lewis Itkin in New York City on February 7, in 1936, of Jewish parents. He was exposed to left-wing politics early in life through his parents' involvement in former Vice President Henry Wallace's 1948 campaign as the Presidential candidate of the newly-created Progressive Party.

Wallace was a leading figure on the left of the Democratic party. He had been Franklin D. Roosevelt's Secretary of Agriculture and second Vice-President, a "progressive" replacement for the conservative John Nance "Cactus Jack" Garner, who famously pronounced the Vice-Presidency "not worth a bucket of warm piss." The handsome Wallace was considered by many the heir presumptive to FDR and the New Deal. But in 1940 he was removed from the Democratic ticket and replaced by Harry S. Truman, who soon succeeded to the Presidency. An Episcopalian, Wallace held that "the church today should be afire with the keenness of its desire to bring about social justice." His interest in mysticism and world religions led him to became a disciple of the peripatetic Russian-born mystic, painter and peace activist Nicholas Roerich.

The new Progressive Party attracted some support among intellectuals. It advocated an end to racial segregation, full voting rights for blacks and universal government health insurance. Wallace refused to appear before segregated audiences or stay in segregated facilities. Unfortunately, Communist sympathizers quickly became the dominant influence in the party which was uncritical of the Soviet Union and advocated a foreign policy acceptable to Stalin. It dissolved after Wallace's defeat and the escalation of the Cold War.

At the age of sixteen, Itkin was ordained a minister of the Peoples Institute of Applied Religion ("The Way"), an organization committed to social activism. Two years later, he was baptised in the Episcopal Church. At about the same time, he discovered the homophile movement, becoming one of the founders of The League, Inc., the New York City affiliate of One, Inc., which later became the New York Mattachine Society. Among *One* magazine's few advertisers was another independent religious order, the Eucharistic Catholic Church. In 1957, the 21-year old Itkin was ordained to the priesthood of the ECC by the head of the Church, Bishop George Hyde. This independent order was the first Christian body in the US to open its ministry to gay people.

In 1959, when the Eucharistic Catholic Church stopped proclaiming a ministry open to gays, Itkin left and with several others formed the Syro-Chaldean United Episcopal Church. This was the first of a number of small radical ecclesiastical groups Itkin founded over the years, including the Order of Divine Love and the Community of the Love of Christ. With these groups Itkin attempted to develop an egalitarian theology centered on "the androgynous spirit of the universal and indwelling Christ," emphasising sexual openness, revolutionary pacifism and universal human rights, and set against high church (often Eastern Rite) liturgy. In this early period, Itkin also made notable contributions to Church history in his writings about the influence of the Jewish temple on early Christian worship. At various times he was linked with radical Mennonites and Sufis. In 1960 he was consecrated a Bishop of the Old Catholic Church by Bishop Jerome Stanley. (The tradition of independent "wandering" bishops is maintained through lineage rather than doctrine.) In the late Sixties Itkin became one of the first Old Catholic bishops to ordain women, a move that led to a major split in his denomination and the loss of most of its property.

"From the early Fifties," wrote Toby Marotta in *The Politics of Homosexuality: How Lesbians and Gay Men Made Themselves a Political Force in Modern America,* "Itkin had riled homophile leaders on both coasts with talk about radicalism, religion, and the importance of expressing homosexual feelings openly." In 1969 he was present for the second night of the Stonewall riots in New York City. He wrote and presented the Resolution on Homosexual Rights adopted by the American Sociological Association, the first such resolution adopted by an American scholarly or professional society. The following year, he and others in the San Francisco Gay Liberation Front famously disrupted the American Psychiatric Convention held in that city.

In their book *Out for Good: The Struggle to Build a Gay Rights Movement in America,* Dudley Clendinen and Adam Nagourney chronicled the event:

> One of the most despised and infuriating figures in all of American psychiatry, as far as homosexual activists were concerned — the author of the 1962 study which suggested that homosexual men were the products of weak fathers and smothering mothers — was scheduled to be on a panel at the [1970] American Psychiatric Convention. Dr. Irving Bieber, by then a

> pinched, ageing figure with a nasal voice, was a magnet for protesters, and the Gay Liberation Front decided to be there too.... Konstantin Berlandt wore a bright red dress and a full beard, and he, Gary Alinder and Michael Itkin, among others, haunted the APA sessions, disrupting them with displays of guerilla theater and angry protests from the floor.

In 1972 Itkin published *The Radical Jesus and Gay Consciousness* and, with his sometime partner Spinstar (Kenneth W. Lundgreen), *Released from Mankind: A Call for Universal Androgynous Community. The Radical Jesus and Gay Consciousness* bears the dedication: "in memoriam Edward Carpenter, Prophet of Gay Freedom." Carpenter, who died in 1929, was an English poet and social thinker who left the Anglican ministry to write about Eastern religions, homosexual emancipation and sex reform. A friend and disciple of Walt Whitman, he helped found the British Society for the Study of Sex-Psychology, a forum for the positive discussion of homosexuality. He lived openly with his partner George Merrill and in the fearful decades following the Wilde trial, boldly and publicly defended homosexuality and gay rights in his books and lectures.

In his 1870 book *Democratic Vistas,* Whitman had written:

> It is to the development, identification, and general prevalence of that fervid comradeship...that I look for the counterbalance and offset of our materialistic and vulgar American democracy, and for the spiritualization thereof. Many will say it is a dream, and will not follow my inferences: but I confidently expect a time when there will be see, running like a half-wild warp through all the myriad audible and visibly worldly interests of America, threads of manly friendship, fond and loving, pure and sweet, strong and life-long, carried to degrees

> hitherto unknown — not only giving tone to individual character, and making it unprecedentedly emotional, muscular, heroic and refined, but having the deepest relations to general politics.

True American democracy, he believed, "infers a new ideal of manly friendship and loving comradeship, without which it will be incomplete, in vain, and incapable of perpetuating itself."

Whitman's English disciple Carpenter followed through in the same spirit: "It is possible," he wrote,

> that the Uranian [gay] spirit may lead to something like a general enthusiasm of Humanity, and that the Uranian people may be destined to form the advance guard of that great movement which will one day transform the common life by substituting the bond of personal affection and compassion for the monetary, legal and other external ties which now confine and control society.

Itkin saw Gay Lib's potential to fulfil Whitman's prophetic dream for America. "Gay Liberation," he wrote,

> is not an organized or monolithic thing. Arising in response to long-felt needs, it consists of many small groups and individuals...cutting across many class and political lines...to whom the life thus far forced upon them is far more to be feared than the penalties to be faced by being open about homosexuality....We are a minority people struggling to create our own subculture. No other minority group, so far as I know, as had this problem. In the process, it is necessary to take note of all the various aspects of our reality and give them expression. The

> immediate issue is that we must continue to intensify the struggle for Gay freedom now and thus create a new Gay Consciousness.

"It must be understood," he explained,

> that the word Gay as used here, while starting from a base of accepting homosexuality, does not exclusively refer to sexual gender preference, but rather defines a life-style in which love, trust and support between all people supplant relationships based on hate, fear and competitive aggression.

In this Carpenterian vision,

> Gay is a process of attaining mutual and equal social and sensual relationships among all human beings." Itkin looked forward to a "true socialism based on the freedom of Women and Gay people...the integral realization of the Self actualized in Community, the restoration of the unity of body and spirit.

"Without too much trouble," he wrote,

> you can walk through the streets of any city in America at almost any hour, day or night, and see the desolate, alienated and oppressed people. Take a moment to talk to adolescent runaways, youth without homes, street people, Black people, Latin American and Indian Americans, the aged, the handicapped, draft resisters, demonstrators for peace and revolutionaries who rightly feel that the institutional church has betrayed the revolutionary message of the Gospel.... While the institutional church

> makes of the scandal of the Gospel a comfortable pew, an alternative Community has in it the possibility of proclaiming the Gospel which is an outrageous shout of Love and Joy!

For Itkin, Gay Liberation entailed the overcoming of evil by the power of love, and the peaceful creation of a new, loving co-operative community that would not only resist power and evil but be an active force for good in the world.

These views place Itkin and his sympathizers in the stream of Gay Liberation that flowed from the hippie counterculture of the Sixties, from earlier American radical social movements (anarchism, the Progressive Party, the peace and civil rights movements, the homophile movement) and from occultism and fringe religions (Jack Nichols had been involved in Baha'i). Other gay-oriented spiritual groups of the time included Troy Perry's rapidly growing Metropolitan Community Church and Robert M. Clement's Manhattan-based Church of the Beloved Disciple.

The significant libertarian/anarchist wing of the early gay movement resisted affiliation to parties or ideologies, but was strongly responsive to the message of Whitman and Carpenter. (Itkin even wrote a full-length, unpublished study of Carpenter.) And as America quickly adjusted to the emerging gay presence, its more libertarian components remained skeptical of both the Democratic Party and the political Left which largely ignored Gay Lib. The Black Panthers enjoyed a brief, unlikely flirtation with the Gay Liberation Front. The (Trotskyist) Socialist Workers Party and its youth wing, the Young Socialist Alliance, dispatched their sexually unorthodox members to report on the new gay movement. Unfortunately for the Party leaders, most of the gay socialists found Gay Lib more compelling than the Party.

Emblematic of the era were magazines like *Come Out!*, *Gay Sunshine*, *The Body Politic* and *Mouth of the Dragon*, books like *The Gay Mystique*, *The Gay Liberation Book* and *The Spiral Path*, the poetry of Emilio Cubeiro, Richard George-Murray and Jimmy Centola, the street art of Ralph Hall, Sidney Smith and Keith

Haring, and the street characters Rollerena and Jon-Jon and Marsha P. "Pay-it-no-mind" Johnson. The on-the-spot theater of Doric Wilson, the music of Chris Robison.

On the New York City scene, lovers Jack Nichols and Lige Clarke edited the important newsmagazine *Gay*. Clarke was a student of Eastern philosophy and a Yoga instructor. Nichols was strongly influenced by Whitman and Carpenter. (He devoted a chapter of his 1996 book *The Gay Agenda* to "Walt Whitman's Vision," remembering that in 1973, gay activists had carried Whitman's *Leaves of Grass* to the twenty-sixth annual Conference on World Affairs in Colorado.) Another Carpenterian was scholar/activist John Lauritsen, co-author of *The Early Homosexual Rights Movement (1864–1935)*; Lauritsen's Pagan Press published an edition of Carpenter's *Iolaus: An Anthology of Friendship* in 1982. A figure from the radical wing of the old homophile movement was columnist and activist Randy Wicker, whose lamp store on Hudson St. was a frequent focus of activities and a haven for activists, artists and street people. (Wicker would support John Anderson's 1980 independent presidential campaign and later became an outspoken advocate of human cloning.)

Based in the Upper West Side, the activist and radio broadcaster Bob "Flash" Storm and his partner, artist Ralph Hall and their rag-tag gang issued *Gay Post, Faggots on Faggotry* and *Ain't It Da Truth,* brightly coloured Gestetnered "gayzines" which they sold or gave away on the street. These self-published periodicals ran poetry by Allen Ginsberg and Robert Burdick, and covered news and events that other media ignored. The *Gay Post* group helped prisoners on Riker's Island and in the notorious "Tombs," and sponsored the Gaywalk, an alternative to the official Christopher Street Parades when they became increasingly commercialized and dominated by organizers with links to the Democratic Party and to organized crime.

The New York Gay Anarchists and their core group the Gay Clone Collective operated out of Hunter College. Rejecting both the "civil rights only" stance of the "gaycrats" and the "Go Red, Go Gay, Go Pick Up a Gun!" rhetoric of the authoritarian left, the NYGA carried their banners to the 1976 Democratic and Republican conventions, and pressed to unite the gay protests there with those of the Yippies. They organized anarchist conferences at Hunter College and New York University and, together with the editors of the gay anarchist zine *The Storm!*, staged a mid-town commemoration of the fiftieth anniversary of the execution of Sacco and Vanzetti.

In Boston, the anarchist-oriented *Fag Rag* collective published its radical gay lib paper as well as books such as Arthur Evans' *Witchcraft and the Gay Counterculture* and the Good Gay Poets series (its name a play on the "Good Gray Poet," Whitman). *Fag Rag*'s most prominent figure, Charley Shively, a poet and professor of American Literature, later published two books on Whitman and his lovers. He was one of the first to discuss Lincoln's bisexuality.

In the West, The Cockettes and the Angels of Light furthered the anarchic tradition of street theater, the eccentric transexual activist Angela Douglas acted as gadfly and provocateur, and the former communist and Mattachine founder Harry Hay, an initiate into American Indian spirituality, encouraged the Radical Faeries. Harvey Milk, the San Francisco councillor assassinated in 1978, acquired his libertarian outlook early — prior to his participation in the Goldwater-for-President campaign of 1964.

Itkin often acted as the spark connecting these disparate groups and individuals, the artists and the activists, the old homophiles and the young gay radicals, the spiritual and the political. A series of Anarchist and Gay Academic Union conferences focused the high spirits of the time, a youthful eroticism energizing the gatherings. Gays, anarchists, bohemians and artists often act as cross-pollinators of cultures, ideologies and eras.

During the '70s Itkin divided his activities between San Francisco and New York City where he was for a time editor of a smudgy gay tabloid called *Maverick*. Under his editorship, *Maverick* mixed city reporting, bar news, articles on gay historical figures, detailed accounts of ecclesiastical quarrels, and contributions by such independent voices as Jim Kepner, Randy

Wicker, Wallace Hamilton, Fred Halsted, and John Lauritsen.

I first met Itkin in New York City in the mid-Seventies. His reputation had preceded him: he was remembered for his amazing multiple orgasms and his tendency not to return borrowed books. On our first encounter, he was hurrying to a conference and we shared a five minute cab ride, during which he propositioned me, suggesting that we would probably be able to find a convenient corner somewhere for a quicky, presumably during a break in proceedings. As this didn't interest me, I let him out at his destination and continued on my way. Itkin seemed unbothered by my demurral and whenever our paths crossed, he was always friendly, voluble, and intense. He displayed little of the pastoral manner, his combative, provocative nature tending to stir up troubled waters rather than calm them. Any networking skills he may have had were not obvious. He worked very hard — or at least, expended a great deal of energy, much of which dissipated itself through lack of focus. His mood swings and uncertain attention span were apparently awarded a medical diagnosis, one which allowed him to draw a small pension, virtually his only source of income (unless one credits the tales of his selling ordinations to nervous clergymen unconvinced of the validity of their own Protestant orders).

He was highly intelligent, and his sincerity was obvious. But his keen mind always seemed overloaded, jumpy, as though some isolated malfunction kept sparking, or jamming, the circuits.

Independent bishops have traditionally been known as "wandering bishops" but Itkin seemed more of a rushing or whirling bishop. A diminutive man of high energy and high spirits, he skittered about like a tiny whirlwind, stirring up controversy as he spun from here to there. By nature a contrarian — seldom a good thing in a bishop — and somewhat unpredictable, he was something of an imp of the perverse. He could provoke people to action, without necessarily staying around for the follow-up. Though lineage and titles were obviously important to him, he seemed perennially unable to decide what to call the various groups, organizations and churches he founded, their complicated names displacing one another in quick succession.

He could be exasperating, and in spite of his playful aspect, could inspire visceral dislike. In his bitterly funny memoir *Dropping Names*, novelist Daniel Curzon reviled Itkin as "a self-anointed little bloated toad," speculating that he probably pissed out of windows. Curzon's recollections of his fellows tend to range from the unflattering to the abusive, and his assessment of Itkin was apparently based on what was at best a passing acquaintance.

I once caught a glimpse of the peripatetic bishop as I was walking through the East Village. A street demonstration was in progress — not a gay demo this time but a local protest, perhaps about housing conditions or squatter evictions. A motley crowd of peaceful protesters faced a armed phalanx of police. In the gap between them was my friend Ralph Hall, a lanky, sweet-natured hippie with a perverse sense of humor. Ralph was crouching down approaching the cops, lips pursed, hands outstretched, cooing "Here piggie piggie piggie!" The police were starting to get restless and blue in the face and Itkin might well have worried that the whole thing could quickly degenerate into a police riot. Grinning, he shook a finger in Ralph's direction, saying "You're a provocateur, Ralph! A *provocateur*!" They both laughed at my wisecrack, "Better a provocateur than an *agent provocateur*!"

Itkin's responses often took people by surprise. At a New York meeting of the Gay Academic Union Scholarship Committee which he regularly attended, Itkin read a copy of the poem that caused Britain's *Gay News* to be convicted of blasphemy, James Kirkup's "The Love That Dares to Speak Its Name," about a Roman soldier's erotic response to the crucified Jesus. Itkin and a woman colleague, according to John Lauritsen, "began sobbing uncontrollably. Mikhail explained that he had never read anything so moving, and that the poem expressed his deepest religious feelings."

Things were changing rapidly — for us as well as for American society as a whole.

The Vietnam war remained the big issue and Konstantin Berlandt's declamatory poem "Bring the Beautiful Boys Home" published in the Ramparts Press anthology *The Gay Liberation Book* was emblematic. But the marches, parades and Gaywalks could never quite decide whether they were a party or a protest. They were both of course, which made them so exciting and hopeful. And through it all, the Bishop would periodically whirl, wobbly and unpredictable as a spinning top, alarming as a dust devil, scattering open letters, ordinations, denunciations and manifestos — and conferring benedictions of Peace Eternal.

By the mid-Seventies the movement was beginning to enjoy some amazing successes even while being rapidly commercialized and co-opted. In October 1973 the GAA Firehouse, symbol of the exuberance and delight of the early movement, burned down amid dark rumours. Only *Ain't It Da Truth* blew the whistle but by that point there were plenty of discos to dance in. By December of '74 Gloria Gaynor's "Never Can Say Goodbye" was the big hit; the party, the sex clubs, and the party drugs, were in full swing. By June 1976, the front cover of *Vector* magazine ran the question IS GAY LIB DEAD? (Inside, everyone agreed it was not.)

In 1977 Itkin moved to San Francisco where he was active in Libertarians for Gay Rights and co-founded the Committee of Concern for Homosexuals which established the first gay help-line switchboard in the San Francisco area. A "Special Issue" of a mimeographed periodical *The Gay Anarchist,* edited by Itkin during this period conveys something of the flavour of his manifestos, written on the fly as they were. *The Gay Anarchist* was the newsletter of the Libertarian-Socialist Gay Caucus (Gay Anarchists), one of the many small (sometimes three-person) organizations Itkin founded to spread the word. The long, difficult-to-remember name with its characteristic parentheses identifies it as a classic Itkin creation, even without his cryptic salutation "BARAQAU BASHAN!"

In the text, which includes his "Open Letter to 'The Movement'" Itkin announces his resignation as editor of *The Gay An-*

archist and as Pacific Coast Convenor of the Libertarian-Socialist Gay Caucus (Gay Anarchists), and shares some of the fruits of his constant self-searching. He writes of allowing himself to "become involved (as so many of us have)" in what he calls "radical traps" — diversions from the "True Aim and... Magnum Opus of the Divine Spirit." He mentions as particularly dangerous "the trap of the conditioned intellect" and its stifling of the independent, liberated mind and heart.

In his "Open Letter," Itkin expresses his frustration with what he saw as the relentless negativity that too often characterised large sections of the Movement. "The only unity one ever finds within the Movement," he sometimes felt, "is unity concerning what it's against. When it comes to questions requiring positive energy, the Movement is not only fragmented, but steadily at odds with itself." He regrets the lack of co-operation in developing community institutions as spiritual oases, alternatives to and refuges from the oppressive social status quo. Such alternatives, he believed, can only develop and thrive if they are grounded in self-realisation, self-actualisation, and honest interpersonal relations. Itkin saw personal encounter with "the True Self, the Divine" as the foundation of any productive work for "one's self, one's community, for all of humanity and for generations yet unborn." This, he added in a wry warning, "is far less glamorous than sitting around at meetings bitching at one another, vying with one another for the media limelight, or indulging in sleep-walking fantasies of violent revolution."

The Open Letter announces Itkin's withdrawal from active membership in many political groups in which he was involved, the better to concentrate on spiritual activism with another roster of organizations that included Peacemakers, the Order of the Great Companions, the Movement for a Pacifist Church of Christ, the World Fellowship of Faiths, the Gay Alternative Outreach, the Gay Caucus of the Society for Social Psychology and the Gay Academic Union Scholarship Committee.

Itkin had paid more than his dues as a Movement radical and agitator for political and social change, but realized that he should not — could not — go for too long without immersion in more Cleansing Waters. "True liberation is a matter of consciousness transformation," he concluded. "We must end our collective sleep-walking state [and] ...awaken to our True Identity...the Divine Love in which we move and have our Being."

From his new base in California, Itkin continued his mission. In 1980 he ordained the novelist Marion Zimmer Bradley and her husband Walter Breen (as "J.Z. Eglinton," the author of *Greek Love*). Other close colleagues there included Itkin's successor Marcia Herndon, journalist and archivist Jim Kepner, who preserved some of Itkin's papers, and Dusty and Kelly Verity — half-sisters and long-time partners, former circus performers who became prominent in S/M and Leather organizations. (In later years, Dusty and Kelly would acquire new names — and new genders.) It was Dusty who, one day when we were discussing her old friend, posed the rhetorical question, "What *is* an itkin, anyway?"

It did seem that at so many events of the time, from Stonewall to the GAU conferences to the latest scuffle in the East Village, Itkin was there, at least momentarily, as instigator, participant, consecrator, and witness.

Mikhail Itkin died August 1, 1989, from complications of AIDS. At his memorial service, according to Rev. Daniel Stouder, "most who spoke "freely acknowledged Mikhail often did not seem to know where he was going, and stories of sexual indiscretion circulated just beneath the surface. His correspondence and journals are filled with backtracking and 'corrections' of earlier positions, frequently accompanied by bitter denunciations of those who still held these now repudiated positions. Yet all agreed he tried to go toward the good and to serve God and Humanity, even during his last debilitating illness."

The Radical Jesus and Gay Consciousness is both a political document very much of its time, and a spiritual record valid for any time. It is an account of Mikhail Itkin's ongoing struggle to reconcile the tortuous complexities of Christian theology with the pressing spiritual, social and sexual needs of his own people. A non-Christian might ask: Why spend the energy? Doctrines as elaborately anachronistic as Immaculate Conception,

Dormition, Resurrection and blood Atonement are obviously irreconcilable with a modern world view. Why not dump the whole baffling Christian conundrum and just get on with it? But any attempt to answer *that* question must first ponder the fact of Itkin's profound engagement with the myth and legend of Jesus — an engagement far from unique to him. That Itkin's efforts toward this cross-cultural reconciliation (unsurprisingly) never quite succeed is evinced by his perennial additions, contradictions, revisions, and politico-theological arguments with imaginary opponents. But, for better or worse, he never gave up, and his partaking in the ritual of Holy Communion each and every day of his life anchored him in both past and present as perhaps nothing else could.

So what is an itkin? An Itkin is Bishop Mikhail Francis Augustine Itkin, a tough little Jewish kid from the Bronx, who believed in his fellow man — and woman, for he always worked with and befriended women as they befriended him. And he believed that ultimately, one's rights on this Earth and one's duties are the same in the Mind of God. His mission as he saw it was to act on those beliefs. A small bishop in a leather jacket, whirling like a dervish through the puzzled crowd.

Bishop Itkin's ashes were scattered in the garden of the Episcopal Church of St. John the Evangelist in San Francisco. In 2002 he was elevated to sainthood by the Moorish Orthodox Church. I suppose whether Mikhail Itkin is a saint or not depends on what house of worship you go to. But he was certainly a brother. Brother Mikhail. God bless.

Editors' note: "What Is an Itkin Anyway?" first appeared in *The Gay & Lesbian Review Worldwide.*

The Passion of Mikhail Itkin

Rosamonde Miller

One Sunday morning, approximately 25 years ago, a bearded man in full black Orthodox regalia that included a tall bishop's hat, veil, pectoral cross and staff, walked with great dignity into our small Gnostic Sanctuary, located at that time in Palo Alto, California. I had just begun giving my regular talk on the keynote for that date leading into the Eucharist service. Although small in stature, he was impressive to say the least. After allowing a few seconds for the bishop to settle himself and for people to recover their composure and stop pretending not to stare, I continued my talk.

During the twenty minute talk he kept his eyes closed in concentration, occasionally nodding in approval. After that, the rhythmic cadence of the Eucharist carried us in its flow. At the time for communion, as is our practice, I invited everyone to partake without exclusion, if they so desired: "The Holy of Holies is uncovered, and the Bridal Chamber invites us in." With great reverence, the bishop came to the altar and received communion.

After the Eucharist he waited for me to finish greeting the people so we could sit down and talk. He introduced himself as Bishop Mikhail Itkin. He had heard of my episcopal consecration some two years earlier, in January 1981, at the hands of Bishop Stephan Hoeller. He and +Stephan Hoeller had maintained some correspondence in the fifties and each had been independently acquainted with Richard, Duc de Palatine (Ronald Powell), who had also been +Hoeller's consecrator.

Recently, +Mikhail and +Richard had exchanged their respective lines of apostolic succession in Los Angeles, hence Mikhail's interest in meeting me, as we shared some of the same episcopal lineage.

I don't remember many of those details, because I usually don't pay much attention or give importance to such things. I had not heard of Mikhail from +Stephan before and had nothing to add, as I have kept to myself through the years, thus avoiding politics and the ecclesiastical grapevine of the time. After a few minutes our conversation became more meaningful and personal. He told me that he lived in San Francisco, was gay and had AIDS, but that the government classified him as having ARC, AIDS related complex, to avoid paying the benefits he needed. AIDS was then highly politicized with negative results for the patients, and ignorance was rampant among the population at large. At that time there was little financial help and few of the useful laboratory studies available today. That was before AZT, the first approved drug for treating AIDS. Finally, with greater awareness, Mikhail came to be recognized as an AIDS patient and eligible for government aid. This drug turned out to be a dangerously toxic substance, responsible for many deaths.

We immediately hit the right notes with each other. We both had a sense of humor and liked to joke. After everyone was gone, he opened his heart for well over an hour. It was not the details of his story that moved me; it was his vulnerability and doubts, as well as his authenticity and consistency, which completely opened my heart to him. That first day saw the birth of a friendship that lasted until his death, in 1989.

Mikhail did not drive and it was difficult for him to take more than one type of public transportation to visit the Sanctuary. I started driving to San Francisco to meet him regularly. I would pick him up at his apartment in Duboce Street, above a bar called Zeitgeist, and take him to breakfast or lunch. For lunch I would take him to places that he would not normally visit; but for breakfast we often went to his favorite place, El Patio, on Castro Street, where we met and sat with a number of his friends and acquaintances. Meanwhile I was acquiring a firsthand education on San Francisco's political machinery and, in particular, the politics surrounding AIDS.

A few weeks later a young friend became diagnosed with AIDS. He was still in his twenties and was terrified by the news when he asked me for spiritual direction and support. I felt better prepared to work with him thanks to my relationship with Mikhail. Thus began a long list of names whose faces, suffering, laughter and courage remain embroidered in my heart.

Mikhail's was an indomitable personality; his determination to survive carried him through the worst moments; even at those times when fear would suddenly strike him and he'd call me in the middle of the night, "Sorry, Love, for calling you so late—or is it so early?" There were others he also called, I'm just glad that I could be available at those times.

Mikhail wanted to live and was doing everything possible to care for himself. Among other things, he began taken homeopathic remedies, especially Bach Flower Essences. Whenever we went for lunch he would bring ten or twelve little bottles that he would line up in front of his plate. At a determined moment, he would measure the drops prescribed for him. There were not enough funds at his disposal for his needs, so we decided at the Sanctuary to pass him a small monthly check out of our donations to help him obtain his alternative medicine supplements.

Mikhail was one of those rare individuals that one senses belonged to an underground type of humanity. He spoke his mind and forged ahead armed with his convictions; he was however willing to shift directions and admit it to others if he saw the subject from a different perspective. This he did with the same passion and honesty as before.

Our conversations focused mostly on his spiritual and ethical perceptions. He had a vast knowledge of theology and politics and would not suffer gladly any person who would present a position without being able to support it with solid arguments.

Mikhail's relationship with God was an uneasy, but very real one. One time we attended the funeral in Berkeley of another friend claimed by AIDS. His name I believe was Kelso. As many people stood up and spoke about the deceased and of their personal experiences with him, Mikhail stood up and with a stentorian voice proclaimed, "God is a murderer and a thief!"

Everyone was stunned, but it was not surprising to anyone that truly knew Mikhail. In his voice was the cry of humanity confronting the traditional belief in a relentless and unyielding God, before whom all are powerless: Broken, at last, were the last vestiges of a belief which, on that day, perhaps he thought paralleled the Stockholm syndrome, in which hostage humanity becomes sympathetic with its captor. He voiced what many who are religious dared not admit even to themselves; the sense of unfairness at a life so young being cut so soon. There in his voice was all the pain and bewilderment that humanity has felt in the face of tragedy and loss, finally breaking into anger, "God is a murderer and a thief!"

We left the church after the service. Mikhail was quiet for a while. Then we went to a restaurant and during the meal he became reanimated. He spoke of Christ and the equality, mercy and love his incarnation came to teach. We spoke about death and about how everything that is born must die. A truth that, when in the face of it, Mikhail found devoid of any solace and that he was determined to fight and postpone with every ounce of his will.

Whenever Mikhail embarked on some new project, his health improved. He enjoyed attending and participating in ordinations and consecrations. I went with him to a few of those, but as a spectator and a guest, not a participant. When there was no new project, he would become outraged about something or someone and would write many letters on the subject. Some people claim that their health improves with relaxation, meditation and visualization techniques. Not for Mikhail. Whenever his T cells where low, if he found something worth fighting, he'd go to battle. The more he battled the more his health seemed to improve. We used to joke about that. His passion was therapy for him.

I was becoming used to Mikhail's sudden enthusiasms and impulsiveness. A friend of mine who had been a Roman Catholic seminarian and was now a deacon in +Stephan's church in Los

Angeles, was in the Bay Area for the day. He called me early that morning asking if he could visit with me later that day. I was already committed to meeting Mikhail for lunch, but I knew that Mikhail wouldn't mind if I brought a friend. They hit it off immediately. I will call my friend Theo, for confidentiality's sake, as I never found out if he ever came out. When it was time for me to leave, the two of them decided to remain visiting for a while longer. A few hours after I left them, they called me up, giddy with excitement. Mikhail had ordained Theo that same afternoon. I didn't know what to say. That morning, before Theo met Mikhail, he had no plans to sever his relationship with +Stephan's church. A few hours later and he had already been ordained to the priesthood by another bishop!

Theo was ecstatic about being ordained a priest after many years of trying. He asked Mikhail to visit him at his home and small chapel in Central California. In spite of their original enthusiasm, their ecclesiastical relationship did not last long. I don't remember the details of their breakup, as I'm allergic to drama of any kind and, as usual, did not pay much attention to the details. What I remember are Mikhail's letters to Theo and others. At the time of the breakup, Mikhail's latest tests showed that his T-cells were too low, almost non-existent. As soon as he became full of fury and began pouring everything he had in letters to everyone he thought should know, he started to become stronger. The angrier Mikhail got, the healthier he became. This was also demonstrated by the much improved results of subsequent blood tests. Mikhail and I continued to joke about how getting angry had a curative effect on him. But anger did not control him; rather, it was a tool that kept depression at bay.

Mikhail sent copies of those letters, as well as writing letters on different subjects directly to Pope John Paul II with copies to different members of the curia, including Cardinal Joseph Ratzinger, now Pope Benedict XVI. I asked why he thought they would be interested, but he did not have any logical answer to that. I'm sure that, to him, his answers were very logical. Very likely that was the very early beginnings of dementia.

To my dismay, he continued writing letters to Rome, mentioning my name in almost all of them. It didn't help that he always wrote of me in very complimentary terms. I was confident that nobody would pay any attention to the doings of some heretical bishops in a country known for its many new religions as well as off-shoots of old, established ones. Still, I did not relish having my name sent to the head of the Inquisition, called in more modern terms, *Congregatio pro Doctrina Fidei,* or Congregation for the Doctrine of the Faith (CDF). I just hoped that they were ignored and destroyed, as I fully expected, at some level way below under-under-under-undersecretary.

Mikhail found solace in classic music and his little old cat, who died shortly after Mikhail. Every single time we spoke he had the classic music station playing on the radio. It filled his tiny apartment with light and sound. When that alone did not do, Mikhail would bring his spirited complaints to God and to any government, religious institution, or person that would get in his cross-hairs, but I never knew him to whine or indulge in useless self-pity. No "poor me" for Mikhail when "damn the SOBs" could do a better job. I admired Mikhail's spirit. If someone asked him what he felt about death, he would reply sardonically that life was a final test and that no one has every flunked at dying.

During my visits to Mikhail I had the opportunity to meet some of his friends. One name stands out among them, Bishop Marsha Herndon. She was an intelligent, caring woman that graced Mikhail's life with her loyalty and friendship.

Most friendships run into some bumps along the way, especially with Mikhail, as I have heard others tell it. That was not my experience. Never a cross word passed his lips. Not only that, but there was never the slightest sour note between us in the years I knew him. We would discuss theological and political points from different angles, sometimes passionately, but it was always with respect and affection. When we could not agree on something, we would laugh and laugh. Laughter too had a curative effect on him. There was always joy in our meetings, even at the saddest times.

It was his love of justice and compassion for the poor and the oppressed that made him sometimes appear more harsh and intransigent than he actually felt. That and not suffering fools gladly made some people become angry at him, at least temporarily. He had suffered much in his youth due to self-righteousness and homophobia. Not the least of his pain was a daughter he lost due to his being gay. His wife was a lesbian, and her parents—I don't know if his parents were involved in this as well—had a court declare them unfit to be parents. In later years he tried to contact her, but she didn't want to have anything to do with her father.

There was a larger other side to Mikhail that more than balanced his combative persona. He was a sensitive and very loving person who cared deeply; too deeply perhaps for his own peace of mind. He had also these flashes of uncanny accurate perception of things he had no way of knowing in any other manner. He also had untapped artistic talent. Mikhail's thoughtfulness showed itself in many little details. I still hang at our Sanctuary a copy of a picture from the XII century of Mary Magdalene proclaiming the risen Christ to the other apostles. In spite of having been very ill and weak, on Eastertide 1986 he presented me with this gift. On another occasion, he drew from intuition a likeness of The Lady, my consecrator in the Holy Order of Miriam of Magdala in France. I also have a beautiful drawing of the Tara he made and framed for me, among various other thoughtful tokens of friendship.

Time was running out for Mikhail. Progressively I became more and more aware of the decline of his mental faculties. The loss of his intellect frightened him more than the prospect of debilitating illness and death. He was very conscious of the process, as day by day he would lose blocks of memory. Mikhail loved to read and now he couldn't finish a page without forgetting the beginning and having to start again from the top. Very understandably, he was frustrated and afraid. The decline was very rapid.

I had not seen him for a few days when I found out he was in the hospital. When I saw him, I could barely contain my tears seeing that face on a pillow that reminded me more of a delicate icon, with eyes disproportionately huge as his body shrank. He was pale and his cheek bones had became more prominent. An ethereal beauty had emerged in his face and a faint light glowed around his head. I knew that was the end. Some days later, I received the news of his death.

One of my sad regrets in life is that I couldn't be with Mikhail in those last days. I was very sick for a few weeks and, when I recovered, Mikhail had already died. My last image of him was seeing him, laying in his hospital bed, and looking into his eyes as if looking through the eyes of an icon.

I had recovered in time to attend his funeral. The church was full to overflowing. His many friends and acquaintances were there to pay their last respects and to say something about his life. I could not say a word. The powerful, troubled and complex being that we knew as Mikhail during that interval between birth and death was finally at rest.

What I remember most of Mikhail's funeral is the moving and profound ritual of release conducted by +Marsha Herndon, which she kindly gave me permission to use freely. After editing and adapting it for the Sanctuary with credit to +Marsha and the Community of the Love of Christ, I used it for the first time in 1989 at the Feast of All Souls in memory of Mikhail. I reproduce it below as close to the original as I remember:

We release you Dear Mikhail and let you go.

We release you and ourselves from any expectations, false images or impressions that you may have had of us or that we may have had of you.

We release you and ourselves from all petty disagreements and unpleasantness that may have passed between us.

We acknowledge the ways in which you touched our lives and the lives of others and the way in which we have touched yours.

We release you from any earthly obligations and responsibilities, worries and cares, pain and strife, misunderstandings and harmful patterns of this life.

We acknowledge that you were a natural expression of God and that you had what naturally comes from being fully human; and that you tried, always, to walk in beauty.

We acknowledge that you always tried to serve God to the degree you were able.

We acknowledge that you always sought God and tried to act to the best of your ability.

We acknowledge all that you did for the sake of love and compassion for others.

We thank you for all the strength and wisdom that we have gained from having known you. We hope that we have, in some way, brought some of the same to you.

May all our sorrows and tears dissolve into healing, serenity and blessing.

May the truth, wisdom, understanding and compassion of the Divine Presence, Redeemer, and Beloved of our hearts, shine always upon you.

May the love of Christ and the Holy Spirit guide you all the way on.

Go forth in Peace, at one with all existence. Amen.

We celebrate life in communion. Let it be, and so it is.

14 January 2008

Mikhail Itkin: The Ecclesiastical Context

John P. Plummer

> ...the gift of love enables us to become in reality what we celebrate as mystery in the sacrifice. — St Fulgentius of Ruspe, "Contra Fabianus," 28:19

The Independent Sacrament Movement As Context for Understanding Itkin

From the time of his ordination by the Eucharistic Catholic Church in 1957 until his death in 1989, Mikhail Itkin primarily presented himself as a Christian clergyperson, although the church within which he served as a priest (and later a bishop) changed its name and theological identity numerous times. Itkin and these various groups belong within the ecclesiastical subculture which has been variously called episcopi vagantes (wandering bishops), Old Catholicism, Independent Catholicism, and Autocephalous Orthodoxy, among other terms. In previous examinations of this phenomenon, I have designated it as the "independent sacramental movement," in an attempt at a descriptive term broad enough to capture the range of groups, orders, and churches, with a minimum of misrepresentation.[1]

By the independent sacramental movement, I refer to a broad range of communities which share a number of characteristics in common: small communities and/or solitary clergy; experimentation in theology and liturgy; mostly unpaid clergy; ordination available to a large percentage of the membership; a sacramental and eucharistic spirituality, with a mediatory priesthood, in most cases preserving the historic episcopate.

These communities trace their history to three primary sources: First, there is the heritage received from the western liturgical churches, beginning with the schism of the church of Utrecht in the Netherlands, breaking from Rome in 1724, and continuing through later splits from the Anglican and Roman communions. Second, there is a significant heritage received from the eastern churches: the Chalcedonian and non-Chalcedonian Orthodox,[2] as well as the eastern churches in union with Rome. Finally, there are important claims to sacramental holy orders which are rooted not in the historic episcopate, but in direct spiritual experience, and non-physical transmission (e.g., ordination received directly from Jesus, the Holy Spirit, the Apostle Paul, deceased Cathar bishops, or an angel).

These historical roots of the movement have been examined in detail elsewhere.[3] For our purpose, it is perhaps enough to note that these various sources have been combined in contemporary independent groups through aggressive cross-fertilization, usually in the form of seeking multiple ordinations and/or consecrations from different sources. There is an intense focus on maintaining the priesthood and some version of the sacramental life, while the churches served by that priesthood and the theology taught by it may be in almost continuous flux.

Itkin's priestly work, and the various churches and orders he created, can be seen as a struggle between two different directions: a radical approach to the Gospel as a program of social liberation, and an esoteric quest for interior transformation and illumination. Contemporary philosopher and maverick Buddhist Ken Wilber has written about the horizontal and vertical purposes of religion, which correlate well with these two emphases in Itkin:

> There are several different ways that we can state these two important functions of religion. The first function — that of creating meaning for the self — is a type of *horizontal* movement; the second function — that of transcending the self — is a type of *vertical* movement (higher or deeper, depending on your metaphor). The first I have named "translation," the second, "transformation."
>
> With translation, the self is simply given a new way to think or feel about reality. The self is given a new belief — perhaps holistic instead of atomistic, perhaps forgiveness instead of blame, perhaps relational instead of analytic. The self then learns to translate its world and its being in the terms of this new belief or new language or new paradigm, and this new and enchanting translation acts, at least temporarily, to alleviate or diminish the terror inherent in the heart of the separate self.
>
> But with transformation, the very process of translation itself is challenged, witnessed, undermined and eventually dismantled. With typical *translation*, the self (or subject) is given a new way to think about the world (or objects); but with radical *transformation*, the self itself is inquired into, looked into, grabbed by its throat and literally throttled to death.[4]

While Wilber's discussion privileges the vertical path of transformation, Itkin never seemed able to settle on either a horizontal or vertical interpretation of the Gospel, being tossed back and forth in an attempt at integration. In both horizontal and vertical paths, Itkin was the heir of his predecessors in the independent sacramental movement, and we will now examine that heritage.

The Horizontal Gospel: Embracing Social Revolution and Inclusivity

Mikhail Itkin is best known for preaching and living a gospel of social revolution and inclusive love:

> Walk down the streets of the city and take a moment out to talk with adolescent runaways, youth without homes, street-people, students and hustlers; with the aged, largely discarded by an affluent society; with women and gay people (male and female) oppressed by the bureaucratic structures and ideology of a sexist society; with black and third world people oppressed by the institutions and ideology of a racist society; with war-resisters and peacemakers who rightly feel that the institutional mainstream churches have betrayed the Gospel of liberation: and know in your gut the alienation of a world-wide cross-section of the people.
>
> It is precisely in this time and place that we are called by the Holy Spirit to participate in the radical lifestyle of love and service to the people taught by Jesus.[5]

He refused to separate the struggle of gay people from that of all other oppressed people, and sought to make common cause wherever possible. According to Itkin, Jesus knew that "all the oppressed people must be united as One (Matt. 5:5) into a world Community (Matt. 13:38) without regard to sex, race, tribe or tongue. (Luke 13:29)"[6]

While Itkin took a more radical perspective than most of his ecclesiastical ancestors, he stood in a long line of independent sacramental churches which had taken ground-breaking stands on gender, race/culture, and sexuality.

Independent sacramental communities began ordaining women to all levels of ministry long before the larger liturgical churches. The first woman consecrated as a bishop in an independent community was Marie Chauvel de Chauvignie, as Tau Esclarmonde, Sophia (female bishop) of Varsovie. Chauvel was consecrated by Jules Doinel, for his L'Eglise Gnostique, in approximately 1892.[7] At this time, Doinel's church did not yet have apostolic succession. Women were ordained in Rudolf Steiner's Christengemeinschaft, from its beginning in 1922, but as with Doinel, this community did not possess traditional apostolic lineage.[8] The earliest certain consecration of a woman as a bishop in apostolic succession is that of Isabel Wilucka for the Mariavite Church, on March 29, 1929.[9]

From the beginnings of the modern independent movement, there have also been groups formed largely to maintain the integrity of their ethnic, racial, and/or cultural group. The Polish National Catholic Church, founded in 1904, was largely a protest against the control of the Roman church in the United States by an Irish and German hierarchy.[10] The African Orthodox Church was founded in 1921 by African American Episcopalians who wanted to assert their independence from a primarily white church.[11]

Most important for Itkin on a personal level — and likely the factor that drew him into the independent movement — was an early openness to gay persons. A number of prominent early 20th century independent bishops (e.g., Frederick Willoughby, James Wedgwood) engaged in homosexual behavior, although it is difficult to know how their sexuality impacted their identity and priesthood. However, a truly revolutionary step was taken by a young independent priest named George Augustine Hyde, on Christmas Eve, 1946. Hyde celebrated the vigil of Christmas in a rented space in Atlanta, Georgia, with a community which was at least mostly gay. As far as I have been able to determine, this mass of the Eucharistic Catholic Church marked the beginning of the very first Christian ministry (of any sort) openly directed toward the gay and lesbian community. Hyde began advertising in the publications of early gay organizations such as *One,* published by the Mattachine Society. Not long after Hyde's consecration as a bishop in 1957, he ordained Itkin, to the priesthood. Itkin eventually denounced Hyde as too conservative, in 1959.[12] In 1960, having left Hyde, Itkin was consecrated to the episcopate for his own independent ministry by bishop Christopher C. J. Stanley of the United Old Catholic Patriarchate of the World.[13]

A priest (later bishop) who also worked with Hyde, Robert Clement, founded the Church of the Beloved Disciple in New York City in 1970. The primarily gay congregation grew to a large size, and served as a model for many other communities. It was Clement at the Church of the Beloved Disciple who appears to have celebrated the first holy union of a same-sex couple in the independent movement in July 1970.[14]

Itkin stood firmly in this long tradition of broadening the boundaries of the church, and pushed it further into the revolutionary change of society. He also made a claim to represent the tradition and jurisdiction of an early independent bishop, Ulric Vernon Herford (1866–1938), who is surely one of the most endearing and genuinely saintly of the autocephalous bishops. Herford was a Unitarian (Liberal Christian) minister, with liturgical leanings. He suffered from the mistaken idea that the Assyrian Church was theologically compatible with his Unitarian views.[15] In 1903, he was consecrated bishop by Luis Mariano Suares (Mar Basilius), a bishop of the Assyrian Church in India. One can only assume that Mar Basilius did not inquire too deeply into Herford's Christology. Herford became a tireless worker for pacifism, animal welfare, and a wide array of social causes. The generally disheveled bishop was often seen bicycling around Oxford, promoting the betterment of all creatures, before returning home to his patient Anglican wife and large herd of cats. Even his detractors noted his sincerity and kindness.[16]

Itkin, like many other independent bishops, had a claim to apostolic succession from Herford, although this did not imply any connection to or authority from Herford's church.[17] He wrote to a bishop in England named William Martin Andrew, whom he took to be Herford's legitimate successor. While Andrew may have had some technical claim in that regard, Herford's jurisdiction (the Evangelical Catholic Communion) was effectively long defunct. Andrew never responded, but this did not stop Itkin from claiming that he had been given authority to carry forward the work of Herford's church.[18] While we might regret the fraudulent nature of these claims, Itkin was, in a true sense, a spiritual successor to Herford in his broad ranging quest for the betterment of society:

> The Creative Spirit sent by Jesus is truly in the world, in the neighbor, in the whole creation – the heart of the struggle against war and division, violence and confusion, sexism, racism, and imperialism: and for freedom, peace, clarity, spiritual unification and human dignity in a universal free Community of sister/brotherhood in the Creative Life.[19]

The Vertical Gospel: Transcendental Liberation

Itkin's focus eventually shifted from an external revolution to change the oppressive structures of society to an inner revolution, bringing his own spirit into conscious union with the spirit of God, in trust that such interior work would provide the foundation needed for external change. In a letter dated September 15, 1977, Itkin confesses that he has allowed himself "to become involved (as so many of us have) in many of the so-called 'radical' traps which divert us from True Aim and from the Magnum Opus of the Divine Love."[20] In an attached "Open Letter to 'The Movement'," he writes:

> But, then, a true Work of Self-realisation and Self-actualisation is absolutely requisite if one is to work for a positive alternative for one's self, for one's community, for all of humanity and for generations yet unborn. And this Work

> is far less glamourous than sitting around at meetings bitching at one another, vying with one another for media limelight, or indulging in sleep-walking fantasies of violent revolution. [21]

This shift in perspective appears as early as 1972, when Itkin writes in the preface to the 2nd edition of *The Radical Jesus and Gay Consciousness*:

> The whole of reality, God included, is evolving and the entire course of its history has been a process of Incarnation, because a new kind of coincidence of Identity is being reached. That true Identity is Christ indwelling all creation and being born anew in manifestation as we become Conscious of the Creative Life-Truth-Spirit.[22]

Sometime in the early 1970s, Itkin had come under the influence of the Armenian occult teacher G.I. Gurdjieff (1866–1949), especially through Thane Walker (1909–1989), a teacher of Gurdjieff's "Fourth Way" system who mixed with minor celebrities and the gay scene in Los Angeles.[23] By the time of his 1977 letter, Itkin was identifying Herford's inheritance from the Assyrian Church of the East with "the Aisors, a Christian sect tinged with Sufism," as described by Gurdjieff.[24] For his publications, Itkin used images, such as the nine-pointed enneagram, which derived from Gurdjieff and his disciples. The clip-art on his flyers also drew from symbols (such as the winged heart) associated with Hazrat Inayat Khan's brand of esoteric Sufism. A flaming cross and sword which appears on Itkin's papers was an emblem of the Discipleship Course of the Holy Order of MANS, an esoteric Christian order active in California in the 1970s.[25]

During this same period, Itkin, although already a bishop, was consecrated (September 13, 1974) by Ronald Powell (a.k.a. Richard Duc de Palatine), an important figure in the resurgence of ecclesiastical Gnosticism. A few years later, he took part in an exchange of consecrations (August 31, 1980) with Michael Zaharakis and Harold Freeman. Zaharakis was interestingly similar to Itkin in his socialist convictions, ministry to the homeless, prisoners and other marginalized people, combined with esoteric pursuits such as the development of clairvoyance and the study of Swedenborgian teachings.[26] Freeman was an original member of the Science of Man Church, which was the predecessor of the Holy Order of MANS, also known for combining direct service work and an esoteric quest for enlightenment.[27] Independent bishops are well known for the practice of repeated consecrations, often in a quest for multiple claims to an episcopal lineage which would hopefully be regarded as "valid" by others. While such motives may well have been present in Itkin, one might also see here an attempt to make a direct, sacramental connection to esoteric transmissions present within the world of independent bishops.

In his esoteric quests, Itkin also stood in a long line of independent sacramental predecessors. From the late 19th century with l'Eglise Gnostique and Jules Doinel, through the Liberal Catholic Church with its connections to the Theosophical Society and the Christengemeinschaft connected to the Anthroposophical Society, and continuing to the present, esotericism has played a very significant role within the independent movement. Many prominent occult teachers, such as Paul Foster Case, founder of the Builders of the Adytum (ordained priest in the Liberal Catholic Church) and Dolores Ashcroft-Nowicki, director of The Servants of the Light occult school (ordained priest in the Church of the Holy Grail), have had connections to the independent churches, even if not always well-publicized.[28]

In sacramental liturgy, through hieratic ritual which speaks to all of the senses, a living connection to the divine is mediated to the participants, with hopefully transformative effect. At least according to members of esoteric churches, this is not so different from theurgy, or high magical ritual, in which changes in consciousness are effected (at least allegedly) in accord with Divine will. In an apocryphal story told about Bishop Charles Leadbeater of the Liberal Catholic Church, it is recounted that Leadbeater wasn't bothered in the least when he was accused of being primarily a ritual magician, with the mass as his preferred form of magic.[29]

Integration?

In considering Itkin, one is left with a chaotic impression of him moving from horitzontal to vertical (in Wilber's terms), from Eastern Orthodox spirituality to the Mennonite Confession of Faith, from neo-Gnosticism to Gurdjieff to the Gospel as anarchist template for liberation, and back again. His sexual exploits are notorious within the gossip of the independent movement, as are his numerous excommunications and denunciations of former friends. He clearly was a difficult personality, if also a prophet of liberation. Was there any regularity in his life, any integration of the cross-currents, any spiritual axis around which the swirling hurricane revolved?

James Ishmael Ford, formerly an independent bishop and acquaintance of Itkin, and now a Unitarian Universalist minister and Zen teacher, writes as follows:

> …his only continuing spiritual practice seems to have been celebration of the eucharist. Unlike many Independent Catholics, who participate in the eucharist only at those irregular occasions when they can gather a congregation, Mikhail maintained the practice of nearly daily celebration throughout his life. While there are sound theological reasons against the celebration of private masses, the eucharist was Mikhail's only constant spiritual nourishment, and it provided him with all he had of that "regularity" which is a hallmark of spiritual discipline.[30]

I think Ford seriously underestimates the frequency of eucharistic celebration in the contemporary independent sacramental movement, often in the form of private masses as with Itkin. In the anarchic, experimental, prophetic, ever-changing world of the independent movement, it is precisely the practice of the priesthood, especially the celebration of the sacraments, which provides the spiritual heart informing everything else.

The eucharist is perhaps the still point of integration between the horizontal and vertical spiritual paths. It is a potent participation in the self-offering of Jesus for the transformation of ourselves and the world, in both inner and outer ways. Mikhail Itkin was certainly a trickster and "a pain in the butt,"[31] and may have been more than a little mad. But, even in the midst of deep personal confusion and seeming lack of direction, he also displayed in his life the shape of the sacrament he celebrated daily upon the altar: a willingness to give of himself tirelessly, even unto death, for the life and good of others.

Notes

[1] See John Plummer, *The Many Paths of the Independent Sacramental Movement* (2nd ed., Berkeley, CA: Apocryphile Press, 2006). I borrowed the term from references in Richard Smoley's *Inner Christianity: A Guide to the Esoteric Tradition* (Boston: Shambhala, 2002), pp. 224, and the website (c. 2004) of the Christengemeinschaft. Further discussion of the benefits and liabilities of this term can be found in small essays on my blog, http://priestcraft.wordpress.com.

[2] By Chalcedonian Orthodox, I mean the Eastern churches which accept the Christological definitions of the Council of Chalcedon (451), including the Greek and Russian Orthodox, and other jurisdictions in communion with the Ecumenical Patriarch of Constantinople. The Non-Chalcedonian Orthodox include both the Oriental Orthodox (Ethiopian, Coptic, Syrian, Armenian, and Indian) churches, and the Assyrian Church of the East, which use different Christological formulae. Independent sacramental groups make claims to apostolic lineage running back to western missions sponsored by a number of

these churches, as well as schismatic clergy who left their former communions to pursue an independent path.

[3] John Plummer, *The Many Paths of the Independent Sacramental Movement* (2[nd]ed, Berkeley, CA: Apocryphile Press, 2006), 13–37. Also, John Plummer and John Mabry, *Who Are the Independent Catholics?* (Berkeley, CA: Apocryphile Press, 2006), 25–37.

[4] Ken Wilber, "A Spirituality That Transforms," *What is Enlightenment?* (Fall–Winter 1997), available on-line at http://www.wie.org/j12/wilber.asp (October 27, 2007).

[5] Mikhail Itkin, "The Community of the Love of Christ," Pentecost 1976, pp.1–2.

[6] Mikhail Itkin, "The Rebel Jesus," n.d.

[7] See Milko Bogaard's account at http://www.gnostique.net/ecclesia/EG.htm (November 7, 2004). A creed written by Tau Esclarmonde in 1913 can be found at: http://user.cyberlink.ch/~koenig/bishops.htm (November 7, 2004).

[8] Capel, p. 102.

[9] Ward, Persson, and Bain, 223. This might have been pre-dated by the oft-rumored yet never proven consecration of Annie Besant by Charles W. Leadbeater of the Liberal Catholic Church.

[10] Stephen Wlodarski, *The Origin and Growth of the Polish National Catholic Church* (Scranton, PA: Polish National Catholic Church, 1974).

[11] Karl Pruter, *The Strange Partnership of George Alexander McGuire and Marcus Garvey* (Highlandville, MO: St. Willibrord's Press, 1986).

[12] See Gary L. Ward, Bertil Persson, and Alan Bain, *Independent Bishops: An International Directory* (Detroit, MI: Apogee Books, 1990), 199–200. Further information on Hyde can be found on the website of the Eucharistic Catholic Church (Canadian Branch), which is affiliated with Hyde's current jurisdiction, the Autocephalous Orthodox Catholic Church of America, http://www.netministries.org/see/churches/ch04614?frame'N (November 7, 2004), and also in an oral history interview conducted with Hyde by J. Gordon Melton of the Institute for the Study of American Religion on July 6, 2005 (http://www.lgbtran.org/Exhibits/OralHistory/Hyde/GHyde.pdf, October 25, 2007). Hyde is currently living in Belleair, Florida, and is still active in ministry, although quite elderly. I am indebted to Archbishop Al Lankenau of the Orthodox Catholic Church of America in Indianapolis, Indiana, Hyde's successor as head of the OCCA, for further information. Hyde left the OCCA to found the

AOCCA in 1996, due to his opposition to women's ordination.

[13] Ward, Persson, and Bain, 199–200.

[14] Robert Clement is still active in the independent movement, although he now lives in California. Information about his history and current activities can be found on his website: http://www.americancatholicchurch.info/americancatholia.html (October 25, 2007). Prior to Clement's 1970 holy unions, Rev. Troy Perry had already celebrated same-sex unions in the Metropolitan Community Church beginning in 1968. Another early independent sacramental pioneer in this area was Rev. Mario Schoenmaker who celebrated a "covenenat of love" for a lesbian couple at the Church of the Mystic Christ in Perth, Australia, in 1973.

[15] The Assyrian Church of the East is an ancient Christian communion, originally from the area of modern Iran and Iraq, but also found in other regions such as India. It split from the larger imperial church in 431, over Christological controversies surrounding Nestorius, as well as political issues involving Persia and Rome. The Church of the East has often been called Nestorian, but does not regard itself that way, and signed a common Christological declaration with the Roman Catholic Church in 1994. It is most definitely not Unitarian.

[16] See Peter F. Anson, *Bishops at Large* (New York: October House, 1964), 130-155, and George Francis Tull, *Vernon Herford: Apostle of Unity* (Bradford: Bradford, 1958).

[17] The various lineages inherited by Itkin— and the complexities involved in some of the claimed consecrations — are ably treated in Rob Angus Jones, *The Complete Apostolic Succession* (Oakland, CA: Free Episcopal Church, 2004).

[18] Correspondence regarding Itkin's claims, from both Itkin and Andrew, can be found in the archives of the British Orthodox Church in London, England. I owe thanks to the BOC archivist, Gregory Tillett, for alerting me to the letters.

[19] Mikhail Itkin, "The Rebel Jesus," n.d.

[20] Mikhail Itkin, Editorial Letter, *The Gay Anarchist* (September 15, 1977).

[21] Mikhail Itkin, "An Open Letter to 'The Movement'," *The Gay Anarchist* (September 15, 1977).

[22] Mikhail Itkin, *The Radical Jesus and Gay Consciousness: Notes for a Theology of Gay Liberation* (Long Beach, CA: Communiversity West, 1972), vii.

[23] Email correspondence with Marcia Herndon, early 1990s.

[24] Mikhail Itkin, "An Open Letter to 'The Movement'," *The Gay Anarchist* (September 15, 1977).

[25] Comparison with papers from the Sufi Islamia Ruhaniat Society and the Holy Order of MANS, in the author's possession.

[26] See Gary L. Ward, Bertil Persson, and Alan Bain, *Independent Bishops: An International Directory* (Detroit, MI: Apogee Books), 200. Also Lewis Keizer, *The Wandering Bishops: Apostles of a New Spirituality* (Santa Cruz, CA: Home Temple Press, 2000), 48–55, 76–79.

[27] Philip Charles Lucas, *The Odyssey of a New Religion: The Holy Order of MANS from New Age to Orthodoxy* (Indianapolis, IN: Indiana University Press, 1995). Freeman left the Science of Man Church before the later development into the Holy Order of MANS, and later became an independent bishop.

[28] Father Cameron J. Mandrake of the Apostolic Church of the Risen Christ kindly provided documentation of Paul Case's ordination. The BOTA website is http://www.bota.org (June 29, 2004). Bishop Sharon Hart, formerly of the Church of the Holy Grail, confirmed Dolores Ashcroft-Nowicki's ordination at the hands of Bishop David Goddard. The Servants of the Light website is http://servantsofthelight.org (June 29, 2004).

[29] I have been told variations of this story many times, by members of the Liberal Catholic Church.

[30] James Ishmael Ford, "Episcopi Vagantes and the Challenge to Catholic Ministry," (M.A. thesis, Pacific School of Religion, 1992), 35.

[31] James Ishmael Ford, "Episcopi Vagantes and the Challenge to Catholic Ministry," (M.A. thesis, Pacific School of Religion, 1992), 2.

WANTED

:: JESUS CHRIST ::

WANTED: For Sedition, Criminal Anarchy, Nonregistration for the Draft, Crimes against Nature, Vagrancy and Conspiracy to Overthrow all Established Governments by Revolutionary Love.

Dresses poorly. Said to be a Carpenter by trade. Ill-nourished. Has visionary ideas of establishing a free and loving society. Associates with common working people, national and racial minorities, the unemployed, homosexuals and prostitutes. Is often to be found in the company of twelve other highly suspicious men, one of whom, John by name, he calls his Beloved. Alias: "Prince of Peace," "Son of Humanity," "Servant of the People." Bearded. Dark-skinned. Marks on hands and feet as the result of injuries inflicted by an angry mob led by bankers, generals, church officials, educators and other respectable citizens and legal authorities. Although he had been in the custody of the State's rulers of darkness in high places, and had been crucified as a political conspirator, and buried, **He Is Risen and in the Spirit lives amongst the people.**

The Community of the Love of Christ
339 Lafayette Street
New York City, N.Y. 10012

"WANTED: JESUS CHRIST"
ARTWORK BY BISHOP ITKIN 1960, REVISED 1976

To Ian
L'Chaim, L'Shalom,

THE RADICAL JESUS & GAY CONSCIOUSNESS

L'Cherut,
+Mikhail

Notes for a Theology of Gay Liberation
by
Bishop Mikhail Itkin

2nd printing

$2.50 donation requested

THE RADICAL JESUS & GAY CONSCIOUSNESS
TITLE PAGE FROM THE SECOND EDITION
(SIGNED TO IAN YOUNG BY THE AUTHOR: "L'CHAIM, L'SHALOM, L'CHERUT," HEBREW FOR "TO LIFE, TO PEACE, TO FREEDOM")

In Memoriam

EDWARD CARPENTER

Prophet of Gay Freedom

©

Copyright - 1972

BISHOP MIKHAIL ITKIN

c/o Radical Gay Christians

Congregation of Jesus our Brother

1326-3/4 North Van Ness Ave.

Hollywood, California 90028

(213) 462-9331

2nd edition

Published by Communiversity West

David Barker, General Editor.

California State University

Long Beach

The Radical Jesus & Gay Consciousness

Dedication Page from the Second Edition

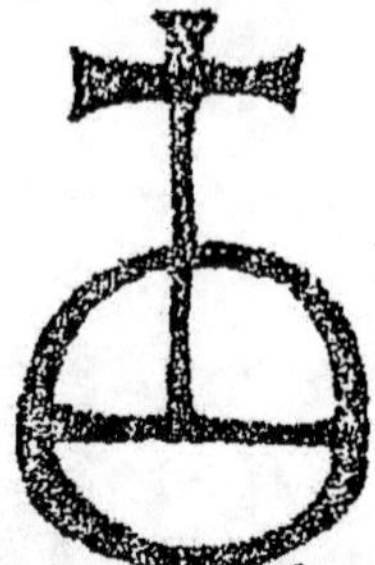

Cross above the Orb

Since the early days of the "Holy Roman Empire," the "Cross above the Orb," sign of the triumphal church, has signified, American Opinion to the contrary, that the whole world is subject to the majesty of Christ. The Peace Cross is a slight modification of that ancient sign, but signifies a radical departure from the days when the Church marched at the command of kings and governors. It is the sign of the liberated church.

Peace Cross

PEACE CROSS ORB FROM *THE RADICAL JESUS…*

The Community of the Love of Christ

"Love is the Spirit of this Community and Service is its Work. And this is our Way: to live together in Peace, to seek the Truth in Love, to help one another in Joy." (St. Basil the Great)

The Community of the Love of Christ is an Ecumenical Religious Order for the spiritual renewal, consecration and transformation of Humanity through the restoration of the Way of Living of the apostolic and primitive Church Catholic. We are committed to radical Christian discipleship, in which the proclamation "Jesus our Brother is Christ, Lord and Liberator: Who died, Who rose, Who comes again!" is central because of its truth and its liberating and motivating power in people's lives. The Good News is the entrance of Jesus Christ into history, the inbreaking of a free and loving community of sister/brotherhood, the proclamation of a message of reconciliation, liberation and new life. The message of Christ and the Kingdom of God—the Liberated Community of Love—brings radical change to human life and society.

We are called to proclaim to all the world the Gospel of Jesus our Brother and Liberator as the Call to make us free: "to bring the Good News to the poor; to proclaim liberty to the captives, new vision to the unseeing, freedom to those in bondage, liberation to the oppressed, the time of the Lord's favor to all" (St. Luke 4:16-17).

The Christ-Truth, the essential Teaching of Jesus of Nazareth, is the Good News of liberation, of freedom for all people. There can be no doubt of that if we carefully read the statements of Jesus preserved in the Gospels and in the apostolic writings of the period immediately following the earthly life of Jesus and through the first three centuries. There can be no doubt as to the Teaching of Liberation, regardless of what mainstream institutional christendom has done to suppress the liberating Truth since 325 A.D. That Good News of liberation—the Gospel of Jesus—is speaking to us today. It is vital for freedom today, just as it spoke to and was vital to the liberation struggle of the "despised and rejected" of Jesus' own day.

Jesus said, "I am come that they might have life, and have life more abundantly" (John 10:10). The Community of the Love of Christ is a covenant-fellowship, an ecumenical Order seeking to help the larger undivided church of which we are a part (and we refuse, as a matter of conviction by the Holy Spirit, to recognise "denominational" divisions in that One Body), to find new ways to serve the people with the Good News of the "life more abundant"—the Gospel of the Kingdom of God in Christ Jesus—in this present age.

Walk down the streets of the city and take a moment out to talk with adolescent runaways, youth without homes, street-people, students and hustlers; with the aged, largely discard-

A RADICAL GAY CHRISTIAN ECUMENICAL ORDER

TO BRING THE BREAD OF LIFE TO THOSE WHO HAVE BEEN OFFERED NOTHING BUT THE STONES OF REJECTION, NEGLECT AND OPPRESSION+++++++

FROM *THE COMMUNITY OF THE LOVE OF CHRIST,* PENTECOST 1976

2 ed by an affluent society; with women and gay people (male and female) oppressed by the bureaucratic structures and ideology of a sexist society; with black and third world people oppressed by the institutions and ideology of a racist society; with war-resisters and peacemakers who rightly feel that the institutional mainstream churches have betrayed the Gospel of liberation: and know in your gut the alienation of a world-wide cross-section of the people.

It is precisely in this time and place that we are called by the Holy Spirit to participate in the radical life-style of love and service to the people taught by Jesus. Christians are called to be a people who will throw themselves into the breach between the peace and healing of God and the loneliness, anguish and terror of the world's lost. We are called to stand as a bridge between humanity and God; willing, even eager, to become ground grain, broken bread, crushed grapes, poured out wine to be fed upon by the earth's hungry until those hungry ones can feed directly upon Christ.

Has not God's liberated community of Love in Christ been promised to the poor and lowly? Was not the Liberator of the world a Carpenter and a Convict, Who died the ignominious death of a Political Criminal: but rose again in glory for our sake?

We come together to follow the risen and living Christ, "the same yesterday, today and forever" (Heb. 13:9). We follow in the Way of Christ Jesus, Who is not a temple dweller nor imprisoned in cloistered sanctuaries, but the One Who has broken all bonds and is at work in all creation and alive in all persons. Our spiritual Work is in the midst of the world.

In the Little Flowers of Saint Francis, it is recorded of the Poor One of Assisi's first audience with the Bishop of Rome: "Francis came armed with a parable. 'There was,' he said, 'a rich and mighty king who took to wife a poor but very beautiful woman, who lived in a desert, in whom he greatly delighted and by whom he had children who bore his image. When her sons had grown their mother said to them, 'My sons, be not ashamed; you are the children of a king.' And she sent them to court, having supplied them with all necessaries. When they came to the king, he admired their beauty; and seeing in them some resemblence to himself, asked them, 'Whose sons are you?' And when they replied that they were the poor sons of a poor woman dwelling in the desert, the king, filled with much joy, said, 'Fear not, you are my children; and if I nourish strangers at my table, how much more you, who are my own children.'"

By this, Saint Francis spoke of the restoration of the Teaching and Way of Living of Christ Jesus and the apostolic and primitive Church Catholic. Even so today!

The trumpet sound of Love is blasting against the church walls: to break down those walls and reveal whether any of the Love of God, the Kingdom of God, the Community of Love, is behind those walls. The Call of the Spirit to us today is to become an ecumenical and non-denominational alternative to the mainstream institutional churches—to seek to bring, in our day, the Good News of Christ's liberation to all people.

In order to fulfill this mandate of the Will of God in the Spirit of Christ, the Church must return to its biblical roots and once again become an alternative community of the pilgrim people of God, sojourners in the world—not seeking for acceptance by

FROM *THE COMMUNITY OF THE LOVE OF CHRIST,* PENTECOST 1976

3

mainstream christendom, nor seeking merely to fill its own cash boxes: but becoming a servant community and a prophetic witness that confronts all oppression, greed and violence, speaking Truth to power, confronting "the powers of wickedness in high places" (Eph. 6:12).

While more often than not the mainstream institutional church sells out its Pearl of Great Price, the Gospel of Liberation taught by Jesus, to property, status and social position: an alternative community in Jesus' Way of Discipleship has in it the possibility of serving the people as steward of that Pearl. While the mainstream church often silences its witness rather than lose its position and wealth: such an alternative community has the possibility of true witness in transforming love and service precisely because it has no wealth and no position. While the institutional church trades in the offensive Jesus for a more comfortable model: such an alternative community has the possibility of being the Body of Christ which was taught by Jesus, Who was the Friend of the outcast and the oppressed, the Enemy of all oppression. While the mainstream institutional church makes of the scandal of the cross an idol to be worshipped from a comfortable pew (and so denies the power of the Resurrection): such an alternative community has in it the possibility of being disciples of Jesus and proclaiming the Gospel—which is an outrageous shout of Love that smashes all idols down, purges the temple of moneychangers and rends the veil of the sanctuary.

The focus of The Community of the Love of Christ must be upon those who are poor, who are oppressed. Christ Jesus is the great Liberator: Who died for us, and rose again, conquering death, that we might live.

Jesus calls all! Jesus calls the oppressed to liberation in the new life; the oppressor to give up the role of oppressor —"sell all you have and give it to the poor" (Luke 18:22)— and in this giving up the oppressor's role, to identify with the people by service. It is in our helping others that we help ourselves the most!

With historic roots in, and episcopate derived from, The Holy Catholic Church of the East and the Apostles through the Metropolitan Province of India, Ceylon, Milapur, Socotra, Messina and the English Missions of The Syro-Chaldean (Aisor) Evangelical Catholic Communion (also known as The Evangelical-Eucharistic Catholic Observance), we come together to restore the apostolic revolution of transforming and liberating Love meaningfully for contemporary humanity; to do the Work of the renewed Christ-Teaching in our age for the spiritual renewal, consecration and transformation of humanity and the world; to fulfill the need of our age for radical Christian discipleship— "Yes, a Christian revolutionary! And not a revolutionary who happens to be a Christian or in spite of being a Christian, but revolutionary because Christian!" (Eric Gill).

We, therefore, strive to become revolutionary Christians, a community of people united in love and dedicated to creating a new world by the grace of God in Christ—a society based on trust, cooperation and sharing. We believe the essential message of the apostolic and undivided Church of Christ to be that people take priority over things or profits, that Jesus' teach-

FROM *THE COMMUNITY OF THE LOVE OF CHRIST,* PENTECOST 1976

4

ings take on meaning only in concrete actions that meet people's material and spiritual needs, and that the church as a community must work on all levels to meet those needs. In the end, God is not for organisations. God is for people! The organisation—the church—is only to bring the Love of God to the people. As Tullio Vinay said, at a Waldensian retreat, "The Church's task is not to save itself—Jesus has already done that. It is rather to give itself in love and service—in fact, to die for the world."

The voice of God in the Spirit of Christ calls to us today—"I am asking for bread: will you continue to give My people stones?"

The world-crisis today demands that the Cross be raised again at the centre of the people's struggle for a liberated and transformed world for all—gay and non-gay; women and men; black, third world and white—and not merely on the steeple of the church. Jesus was not crucified in an elaborate church-building between two candles: but on a Cross between two thieves or political prisoners (crucifixion having been reserved for political "enemies of the state", often called "thieves" by those whose class-privilege they threaten); at the town garbage-heap; at a cross-roads so cosmopolitan that they had to write Jesus' title in three languages; at the kind of place where cynics talk smut and thieves curse and soldiers gamble. That is where Jesus died, and that is what Jesus died about: and that is where the Community of Jesus must be and what the Community of Jesus must be about—the bringing into being a liberated and transformed world, the Kingdom of God on earth, a liberated community of sister/brotherhood in the Love of Christ!

Believing that we must be a part of all struggles for human liberation—Good News to the poor, release to the captives, sight to the blind, liberty to the oppressed—and hoping to help one another grow and find the life abundant, The Community of the Love of Christ welcomes as members all people who share our goals and beliefs and who are willing to take responsibility for making them a reality in the life of the Church Universal.

(The above INTRODUCTION to the Community is excerpted from THE WAY OF DISCIPLESHIP or RULE.)

This Printing
PENTECOST 1976

(This Ecumenical Gay Christian Religious Order is canonically affiliated as a Province of THE SYRO-CHALDEAN EVANGELICAL CATHOLIC COMMUNION, sometimes called Nestorian.)

ΑΓΑΠΗ

THE COMMUNITY OF THE LOVE OF CHRIST
(SYRO-CHALDEAN EVANGELICAL CATHOLIC COMMUNION)
339 Lafayette Street / New York NY 10012
(212) 228-9244

FROM *THE COMMUNITY OF THE LOVE OF CHRIST,* PENTECOST 1976

The Community of the Love of Christ

6326 Lexington Avenue, Suite 120
Hollywood CA 90038
14 April 1977

Libertarian Party
National Headquarters
1516 "P" Street, N.W.
Washington DC 20005

c.c.: Julian Beck; Carl Bissinger; Rt. Rev. Walter Henry Breen, DD; Rt. Rev. Raymond Charles Broshears; Catholic Worker; CLONE; Come! Unity Press; Wayne Dynes, Ph.D.; Rev. Michael Benedict Ferri, C.L.C.; Freespace Alternate U; Gay Anarchists; Gay Post; Allen Ginsberg; Albert L. Gordon, Esq.; Ralph Hall; Craig Alfred Hanson; Industrial Workers of the World; Christopher Isherwood; James Kepner, DGS; Morris Kight; Larry L. Lawrence; Winston Leyland; Libertarians for Gay Rights; Living Theatre Collective; Judith Malina; Rt. Rev. Milton Placidius Malkin, C.L.C.; Rev. Muriel Marushka, C.L.C.; Kate Millett; Martin Nixon; Bob Palmer; Mt. Rev. Mar Paulus, DD; Peacemakers; Rev. Donald Pederson; Rev. Troy D. Perry; Harold Pickett; Frederick Rabenstein; Ralph Raico, PhD; Rev. Kenneth Albert Rau, C.L.C.; John Rechy; Charlie Shiveley; Marcia Silverstein; Rev. Robert Sirico; Social Revolutionary Anarchist Federation; Spinstar; Flash Storm; The Storm magazine; Mark Sullivan; John Vernon; Thane Walker, MD, PhD; Susan Williams; Pete Wilson; Ian Young; File

AN OPEN LETTER CONCERNING
RESIGNATION FROM MEMBERSHIP IN THE LIBERTARIAN PARTY / NATIONAL

Sisters and Brothers--

In re the above-captioned matter, I am writing to resign from national membership in the Libertarian Party. The reasons for this are many, and I shall only deal with the most basic ones in this letter.

I apologize to all of my Anarchist and Communitarian-Libertarian or Libertarian-Socialist comrades for my misguided individual alliance with the Libertarian Party. Believing some of the early literature which described the L.P. as a left/right coalition of libertarians and anarchists, and in the Spirit of reconciliation in the Liberation taught by Jesus, I joined the L.P. as an individual national member.

Although the L.P. claims to be a coalition of right/left libertarians --with positions ranging from Ayn Rand and Ludwig von Mises laissez faire (and even stranger) positions on the far right, to anarcho-socialist and communitarian libertarians on the left--in truth, looking at various past issues of <u>L.P. News</u>, I find very little of a left-libertarian perspective.

Looking at the reality of the L.P.--particularly as it exists in California--it is clear that its makeup is almost completely right-wing

(more)

FROM *THE COMMUNITY OF THE LOVE OF CHRIST,* 14 APRIL 1977

- 2 -

pseudo-libertarian. It is perfectly clear that not one of these proponents of laissez faire capitalism -- nonthinking "social-Darwinist economic 'libertarianism' of the far right" as Ursula K. Le Guin describes it -- have ever realized that the core of true Libertarian-Anarchist thought might be summed up in Proudhon's germinal phrase: "Property is theft."

What such right-wing "libertarians" refuse to recognize is that the State must be opposed in all of its murderous actions. It is the State, regardless of what economic label it operates under, that is the enemy of the freedom of every woman and man alive today; and the destroyer of the ecology so that the State even threatens every generation yet unborn. The sole purpose of the State in its violence and terror is to protect property.

But in their propertarian egoising, in spite of all their rhetoric of "freedom", such right-wing "libertarians" would perpetuate the terrorism of the State--whether by private militias or by the police & military State of today.

Apparently, such right-wing "libertarians" are perfectly willing to use the technique of the "big lie" utilized by every totalitarian State and so popular among our contemporary politicians. Choosing to disregard historic reality, they have pretty well ripped off the term Libertarian: having chosen to lie and distort history. It is a fact that historically the term Libertarian is synonomous with Communitarian Anarchism. It first came into use in Spain in the 1800s, when to call oneself an Anarchist openly meant signing one's own death warrant. It was in perpetuation of that European tradition, that the term was first used in America by Communitarian Anarchists and Anarcho-Syndicalists: e.g. Libertarian League, Libertarian Book Group, etc. In a sense, the term Libertarian, in its historic use, is a closet term for philosophical Anarchists of the left....and to have it ripped off by laissez faire capitalists is a gross distortion of historic reality.

As a radical Gay Christian anarcho-pacifist communitarian, I joined the L.P. firmly believing it to be the broad Libertarian coalition which its early publicity proclaimed it to be. I discovered, to my horror, that this is not the case.

The matter has come to a head over the situation within Libertarians for Gay Rights. Elsewhere than California, LGR is a coalition of Gay and Gay-supportive right/left Libertarians and Anarchists. In California, the Reverend Robert Sirico, a closed-minded neo-fundamentalist and propertarian exponent of laissez faire capitalism, a self-proclaimed disciple of Ayn Rand and Ludwig von Mises (not of the radical Jesus the Liberator who overturned the tables of the money changers); a "Pastor" of one of the establishmentarian, propertarian and egoising Metropolitan Community Churches which rather than serving Gay people with the Gospel of Liberation, instead defuses righteous Gay rage and treats Gay people as so many "sheep" being served up as mutton for the exploiters--became the Chairman of the California Libertarians for Gay Rights. That California L.G.R. is affiliated with the California L.P.: and thus indirectly with the National L.P.

Sirico runs a totalitarian exclusionist group: making it perfectly clear that there is no room for Gay Anarchists, Anarcho-Pacifists (yes, he

FROM *THE COMMUNITY OF THE LOVE OF CHRIST,* 14 APRIL 1977

- 3 -

also justifies military and police force, from a propertarian stance), Communitarian-Libertarians and/or Libertarian-Socialists within the propertarian ranks of his Libertarians for Gay Rights. Likewise, there is apparently no room in the California L.P. for Christian Anarchists, Gay Anarchists, Anarcho-Pacifists, Communitarian-Libertarians or Libertarian-Socialists.

Although many of the problems dealt with above are peculiar to the California L.P. and L.G.R., at least in the extreme form in which they occur here, it is only reasonable to assume that the same are true (although perhaps to a lesser degree) in the LP National and in all of its affiliates. (I know that this is less true of the Free Libertarian Party and Libertarians for Gay Rights in New York, since I know of Communitarian Libertarians and Anarcho-Pacifists in that Party: but that is apparently the exception, not the rule!) Since one of the reasons for joining the L.P. was to enjoy the fellowship and mutuality of other Libertarians and Anarchists, and to exchange ideas freely with others: and since it is impossible under the circumstances described above to do so, I see no reason for retaining membership.

On 4 February 1977, I sent the Libertarian Party - National Headquarters a U.S. Postal Money Order (# 2214060017) for $8.00 as membership dues and subscription to L.P. News. Included was a copy of the National Membership Application.

To date, membership has not been acknowledged nor has the subscription begun.

INSOFAR AS I AM RESIGNING, WITH THIS LETTER, FROM NATIONAL MEMBERSHIP IN THE LIBERTARIAN PARTY, I REQUEST THE IMMEDIATE RETURN OF MY MEMBERSHIP FEE!

Insofar as that membership fee was sent by U.S. Postal Money Order, please return it by the same method: as I do not use banks (cf. Saint Thomas of Aquin, "Usura contra naturam!").

In the nonviolent struggle for the beautiful anarchist-androgynous community of sisterbrotherhood in Christ our Liberator:
L'Chaim! L'Shalom! L'Cherut!

+Mikhail F. Itkin, CLC

The Right Reverend Mikhail F. Itkin, C.L.C.
Episcopal Coordinator: The Community of the Love of Christ
Pacific Coast Coordinator: Libertarian-Socialist Gay Caucus

FROM *THE COMMUNITY OF THE LOVE OF CHRIST,* 14 APRIL 1977

THE GAY ANARCHIST

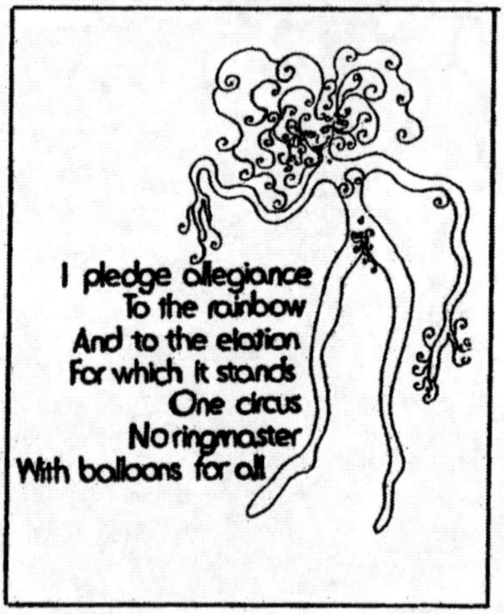

journal of

Libertarian-Socialist Gay Caucus

Published Irregularly **May-June 1977** **Volume I, Num. 1**

75¢ Institutions.
Individuals 40¢ Donation: More if You Can, Less if You Can't.

FROM *THE GAY ANARCHIST,* ISSUE #1, MAY–JUNE 1977

2

"To Realise Freedom!"

"To realise freedom!" That statement by Edward Carpenter sets forth the goal of this journal.

Like most of the world's population today, we Gay people are a colonized people. But there is one quality of our situation which is not shared by any other colonized people -- excepting Women -- and it is the condition which gives the Gay and Feminist struggle for liberation a very special role in the international revolutionary drama. We are the only colonized peoples who are born, raised and mis-educated right in the house of the oppressor. We are all people who have been raised in the patriarchal nuclear family, and only come to find our identity and our struggle as we grow.

Our struggle is crucial within the context of world revolution. We are not only an oppressed people; but being raised in the belly of the beast, we know their lies and their myths intimately. Thus our liberation is the key to the liberation of all oppressed peoples. Only through a nonviolent revolutionary Gay and Feminist movement, united in solidarity with all other oppressed peoples, can we bring about the beautiful free creative community of sister/brotherhood, the androgynous anarchist society towards which we strive.

Our goal, in the words of Jean Genet, must be "to pierce the shell of the world's contempt!"

And yet, we have for too long been a people very easily co-opted by the violent, anti-life, anti-sexual patriarchy: simply because we have been raised in the house of oppression and have internalized the values of the oppressor, in far too many cases. We see the so-called "leadership" of the "Gay Movement" grovelling before politicians -- both hetero and establishmentarian homosexual -- seeking to get crumbs of that toleration which Jean Cocteau put down, when he said: "I don't want to be tolerated. That wounds my love of love and of liberty."

The politicians promise all sorts of "Gay rights legislation"; but there is nothing that they can get for Gay people that wasn't a "Gay right" in the Weimar Republic. And it collapsed into Nazi Germany.

Those who do not learn from history, are doomed to repeat it!

The sell-out of the revolutionary potential of the Gay Liberation Movement was predicted by Carl Wittman in A Gay Liberation Manifesto, first published at the Gay Liberation Conference in Berkeley (December 1969): "As Gay Liberation grows, we will find our uptight brothers and sisters, particularly those who are making a buck off our ghetto, coming on strong to defend the status quo. This is self-oppression: 'don't rock the boat'... 'gay people just aren't together'; 'I'm not oppressed'. These lines are right out of the mouths of the straight (sic) establishment."

The American patriarchy says: "History is over! Fit in. The best system in the history of man -- and it is the man's history, not Gay people's, not Women's, not Humanity's as a whole -- has been discovered: it's yours. Nothing else is possible because humanity is selfish, greedy, tainted by original sin." And if we don't buty that product, don't fit in to that pattern -- and Gays do not -- they lock us up.

But for the masses of people throughout the world, history is just beginning. Gay Anarchists know that we must start again too, rebuilding from scratch.

FROM *THE GAY ANARCHIST,* ISSUE #1, MAY–JUNE 1977

3

Uniting for real alternatives, we come together as a loose federation of Gay Anarchists, Communitarian/Libertarians and Libertarian-Socialists drawn from several diverse groups.

The first Gay Liberation statement, published in New York City, September '69, put it clearly: "Gay Liberation Front is a revolutionary group of homosexual women and men formed with the realization that complete sexual liberation for all people cannot come about unless existing social institutions are abolished. We reject society's attempt to impose sexual roles and definitions of our nature. We are stepping outside these roles and simplistic myths. We are going to be who we are. At the same time, we are creating new social forms and relations, that is, relations based upon sister/brotherhood, cooperation, human love and uninhibited sexuality. Babylon has forced us to commit ourselves to one thing... revolution!" (adapted from Come Out)

Gay is not only good: Gay is beautiful, Gay is glorious! There's nothing that the united strength of Gay people struggling for liberation can't do if we choose. Our strength is built on the long muffled and secluded agonies everywhere, in the histories of each one of us. And when that collides with the liberating joy we never before were permitted, there is a force unleashed that is outlaw and glorious and wild. A force that will change the world!

Most Americans -- Gay or non-Gay -- consider themselves to be neither rich nor poor, neither success nor failure, neither privileged nor deprived. They have been carefully taught that they are simply part of the great middle and that, in a hungry world, they should count themselves lucky for it.

Our present time of crisis proves the falsity of that assumption!

We, at THE GAY ANARCHIST, don't count that as being a "lucky" condition to be in. Those arrogant with power have built a trap; and like lemmings marching to the sea, most people have fallen in. Those arrogant with power despise the true individual (the word means "one who is undivided in him/herself", in its origins), and so they try to keep us too satisfied to rebel, too insignificant to matter.

It's always necessary for the ruling class of the State to keep the people in a sleepwalking state. If they're hungry, quiet them with food stamps. Lull them to sleep with phony promises of security, kill off the spirit of creativity by inculcating standards of propriety and conformity -- and keep a ritual scapegoat to blame when things go wrong. Calm the people...destroy the individual!

And now, as always in the history of the patriarchy, faggots and dykes are the ultimate scapegoat for the State.

But we have seen through this trap. THE GAY ANARCHIST calls out, in

FROM *THE GAY ANARCHIST,* ISSUE #1, MAY–JUNE 1977

4 the words of the ancient prophecy, "Awake and sing, you who dwell in dust ...and the earth shall cast out its dead" (Isaiah).

THE GAY ANARCHIST seeks to end our collective sleepwalking state: to awaken us to our true identity, our individuality which can never be duplicated identically in any other person, and yet is a manifestation of the same One Creative Life of all. We seek the Truth of a nonviolent, free and loving way of life. We recognise the Unity of all life. We proclaim the wholeness of each individual and resist the fear and deceit that separates us from our own inner reality.

Recognising a special connection with all other oppressed peoples of the world and joining them in work for the beautiful nonviolent creative society -- the Commonwealth of All -- we are called out of the robot-like trance of mass conformity. Upholding our true identity as One Creative Life, we commit ourselves to resist the sexism, racism, militarism, nationalism, classism and oppression which are the symptoms of the patriarchy which threatens our future and the future of generations yet unborn.

We proclaim our solidarity with all who hold that "We should not seek to fit into this culture, this dying nation of playboy pinups and stinking rivers. We do not want to prove that we can make better marriages, cops or business men than straights (sic). We owe this culture nothing but our determination to replace it" (Vancouver Gay Liberation Front, 1970).

We seek to build the androgynous anarchist commonwealth of sister/brotherhood. Total Human Liberation is the goal! Gay Liberation is our revolutionary way to that goal.

—Mikhail F. Itkin, C.L.C.

(Submitted as a contribution to the discussion of **AIMS AND PURPOSES** for **THE GAY ANARCHIST** and the **LIBERTARIAN-SOCIALIST GAY CAUCUS**)

++

AFTER CIVILISATION

We are a menace to you, O civilisation!
We have seen you—we allow you—we bear with you for a time,
But beware! for in a moment and, when the hour comes, inevitably,
We shall arise and sweep you away!

—Edward Carpenter

Fear of Love is the Source of All Oppression

FROM *THE GAY ANARCHIST,* ISSUE #1, MAY–JUNE 1977

THE GAY ANARCHIST

SPECIAL ISSUE — 15 September 1977

!!! E D I T O R I A L !!!

An Open Letter to Readers of The Gay Anarchist,
Comrades and Friends of the Libertarian-Socialist Gay Caucus (Gay Anarchists),
Comrades and Friends of the larger Gay Anarchist Movement,
Comrades and Friends of the Social-Revolutionary Anarchist Federation (SRAF),
Comrades and Friends of Freespace Alternate U,
Fellow-Workers of the Industrial Workers of the World (IWW),
Friends and Co-Workers in the Libertarian Party,
and the Anarchist & Libertarian Movement at large!!!!!!!!!!!!!!!!!!!!!!!!

BISMILLAH!

This will be the last issue of The Gay Anarchist which I will be editing. I also hereby withdraw as Pacific Coast Convenor of the Libertarian-Socialist Gay Caucus (Gay Anarchists).

For reasons which, I hope, will be clear to readers of the OPEN LETTER TO 'THE MOVEMENT' which is reprinted in this issue, I am cutting back on my socio-political involvements and devoting my energies to that Work of the Harmonious Development of Humanity and the Earth by which a true nonviolent (r)evolution may be brought about, the Work to which I know that I have been called by the Creative Spirit.

As said in that OPEN LETTER TO 'THE MOVEMENT', in the many years since I first received that Call, and have known what my Work is to be, I have allowed myself to become involved (as so many of us have) in many of the so-called "radical" traps which divert us from True Aim and from the Magnum Opus of the Divine Love.

This letter, therefore, serves not only as my notice of ending the Editorship of The Gay Anarchist and leaving LSGC as Coordinator, but also of my withdrawal from membership in the many organisations of the Anarchist, Libertarian and Gay Liberation Movement as a whole.

I will, of course, as said in that OPEN LETTER TO 'THE MOVEMENT', join with you as an individual in confronting specific wrongs when they occur and in working for the unpredictable good for all of Humanity and the Earth. However, my own way of living must now become one of building the transcendental foundations of true liberation firmly, by the pursuit of the Magnum Opus of the Harmonious Development of Humanity and the Earth in Christ.

Within that framework, I intend to continue in the Work of Light, Love and Liberation: that we may begin to realise and actualise the Transcendent Society, the beautiful nonviolent creative and universal commonwealth of sister/brotherhood in the Creative Life. This Work of the Free Spirit, in which each functions as a responsible being, therefore responsive to our environment and to the needs of Life, will lead us into a holistic future: and to this Work I now rededicate **all** of my efforts.

Therefore, excepting those few groups of universal viewpoint which function around somewhat similar aims, such as Peacemakers, Order of the Great Companions, Movement for a Pacifist Church of Christ, and the World Fellowship of Faiths on the one hand, and those few particularist groups in which I feel I can make a contribution in a disciplined and scholarly manner, from the viewpoint of this Work of Creative Androgynation, such as Gay Alternative Outreach, Gay Academic Union (particularly the Scholarship Committee) and the Gay Caucus of the Society for Social Psychology on the other hand: I now withdraw from the organised Movement as a whole. I remain affiliated with those listed exceptions.

I ask, however, that such Libertarian, Anarchist, Pacifist and Gay Liberation organisations with which I have been affiliated until this time (and which are not listed among the exceptions above), continue me on their mailing (but not membership) lists.

BARAQAH BASHAN!

+Mikhail, ODL

FROM *THE GAY ANARCHIST,* SPECIAL ISSUE, 15 SEPTEMBER 1977

7985 Santa Monica Blvd., Suite 219
West Hollywood, California 90046
(213) 462-0314 ext 120

AN OPEN LETTER TO "THE MOVEMENT"

Sisters, Brothers, Comrades, Friends and Lovers —

This open letter is my **Farewell** to that amorphous conglomerate euphemistically known as "the Movement."

Most of the recipients of this letter are gay. Probably all of the recipients — gay or nongay — consider themselves to be "radical", regardless of how each defines that term. I find, after many years of so-called "radical" activity, that I no longer accept their definition(s) of that term.

The word "radical" means "to go to the root." All self-styled "radicals", and all parts of "the Movement", loudly proclaim that they are working for Human Liberation. However, **the root of Liberation is to be found in our True Self, our transcendental and transpersonal Identity, the Divine Love in which we live and move and have our Being.**

But "the Movement", almost without exception, has been unwilling to do any serious Work towards realisation and actualisation of the necessary conditions for true Liberation. Rather, caught in a materialistic and egoising sleep-walking state, "the Movement" only unites on negative energies (and not even very well then). The only unity one ever finds within "the Movement," is unity concerning what it's **against.** When it comes to questions requiring positive energy, "the Movement" is not only fragmented, but steadily at odds with itself. As a "Movement," there are no constructive efforts being undertaken to provide any viable alternative to what is, on one level, quite correctly perceived as an oppressive society.

But, then, a true **Work of Self-realisation and Self-actualisation is absolutely requisite** if one is to work for a positive alternative for one's self, for one's community, for all of humanity and for generations yet unborn. And this Work is far less glamourous than sitting around at meetings bitching at one another, vying with one another for media limelight, or indulging in sleep-walking fantasies of violent revolution. That trap of the conditioned intellect is all too easy to fall into; and today's "Movement" is every bit as clear an example of that type of materialistic, egoising, and conditioned functioning as the "Anita Bryant / John Briggs syndrome" on "the other side".

Of course, there are obvious injustices to be countered. Of course, there are negative events to be dealt with.

But it is essential, if Energies are to be transformed in such a way that we may truly begin to realise and actualise the Transcendent Society, the beautiful nonviolent creative and universal commonwealth of sister/brotherhood in the Creative Life, that each of us takes full responsibility for her/his own actions, thoughts and feelings. It is of the utmost urgency that we begin to function as responsible beings, therefore responsive to our environment and to the needs of Humanity and the Earth.

But "the Movement", far from doing this and, by so doing, taking the essential evolutionary leap that will prepare us for the future and enable us to bring into being a truly liberated society, is tied to paradigms of violent revolution or liberal reform, which really seek to do nothing but change the rulers, change the class-structures, or change the elected representatives. Tied as it is to structures of the past, "the Movement" has rendered itself worse than useless for any long-range change that will lead us into a holistic future.

I should have realised all of this a long time ago.

Perhaps, on a deep level of my being, I did so: but I have rarely acted upon it.

I first became involved in "the Movement" in 1948, during the Henry Wallace Presidential Campaign on the Progressive Party ticket. All of the reasons were legitimate — world peace, human rights and human dignity, a just social order. Those were also the reasons I became involved in the infant "Homophile Movement" in New York City in 1954.

However, fired up by a misplaced adolescent enthusiasm, I rapidly found myself enmeshed in the usual morass of well-intentioned, self-styled "radical" groups; almost all of which based their analysis (if conditioned, mechanistic re-active patterns can be called "analysis") and their praxis on nothing more than the most shallow materialistic grounds.

I will admit that after I left the shadowy regions of Marxist groups, and began functioning around Anarchist and Pacifist groups, the situation was somewhat better. Occasionally, in those circles, one found some individual who was truly working on him/her-self and had some genuine and creative insights. But for the most part, "the Movement" — every bit as much as the society it opposes —

(more / over)

FROM *THE GAY ANARCHIST,* SPECIAL ISSUE, 15 SEPTEMBER 1977

\- 2 -

despises **the true individual** (the word means "one who is undivided in him/herself"). And so, while the old society tries to keep us too satisfied to rebel, yet too insignificant to matter, "the Movement" tries to keep us simply in a mechanical re-active pattern, functioning **against** those things it opposes, but not building any creative alternatives with our lives by doing any **Work** towards Self-realisation and Self-actualisation. For both the old society and for "the Movement," it's always necessary to find a scape-goat. (For the old society, the current prime scape-goat is the gay community: but it's only the re-emerging latest in a long series of scapegoats.)

Yes, for both the old society and "the Movement", we see the same trap of the conditioned intellect. And, in "the Movement," sad to say, even those with the greatest creative potential have fallen into that trap.

But it is necessary, if we are to ever achieve that liberation we say we are working for, to see through that trap! The prophets of old called out to us: "Awake and sing, ye who dwell in dust... and the Earth shall cast out its dead."

We must end our collective sleep-walking state. **We must awaken to our True Identity,** called in the ancient Traditions the universal and indwelling Christ, the Buddha-Nature, the Beloved, Tao, God in Whom we live and move and have our Being. Within that One Eternal Nature, birthless/deathless, without beginning and without end, ever abiding, we can discover our individuation, our true individuality which can never be duplicated identically in any other person.

In 1960, even while being heavily involved in "the Movement", I was consecrated as Bishop for an Order with a specific Aim and in a specific Work: a Work which had been described by Georgi Ivanich Gurdjieff, the man who introduced Fourth Way Sufi Work to the West as "a religious Order seated near Mount Ararat, the Aisors, a Christian sect tinged with Sufism."

This Aisor Tradition, formally know as the Syro-Chaldean Church of the East, was introduced to the West in 1902, when the **Order of the Divine Love,** founded at Oxford (England) in 1898, received its first Bishop in apostolic succession from that Tradition.

When I was consecrated as Bishop in and for that Work in 1960, it was to renew that Order for the Harmonious Development of Humanity and the Earth in Christ: through the restoration and renewal, in terms suitable to the dawning New Age, of the Gospel Christianity of the Syro-Chaldean (Aisor) Tradition, sometimes called Fourth Way Christianity and sometimes Christian Sufis.

In spite of that clear Aim and knowing this Work to which I have been called, I allowed my early so-called "radical" conditioning to prevail, and I fell into that trap described above.

Now, it is time that I resume a full-time dedication to the genuine **Work of Liberation.**

The ancient **Initiate's Vow of the Christ-Mysteries,** preserved in the **Order of the Divine Love,** describes that **Work** in these words: "I have beheld a Spark of the Divine in Humanity. That Spark, the universal and indwelling Christ, must be nurtured as the flickering ember is shielded from the driving rain, even at the cost of my life."

Out of that commitment, a genuine Work for the spiritual renewal, consecration and transformation of Humanity and the Earth should grow. That requires that we each take on awareness of our own responsibility for our lives, for our community, for the creative evolution of Humanity and the Earth both now and for generations yet unborn.

That **True Identity,** spoken of above, reflects the androgynous nature of **the Transcendental Reality** in Which we live and move and have our being. As such, the androgynous nature of **All-that-Is** becomes clear: and dualities disappear, polarities are resolved into the **One,** and our oppositions and divisions of sexism, racism, nationalism, classism, and so forth are shown as just what they are — the fantastic lies of our sleep-walking state. Awaking from that dream, we begin the actualisation of the Transcendent Society.

As such, I now bid **adieu** to "the Movement", after these many years of dedication to it.

Of course, I will join with you in confronting specific wrongs when they occur. Of course, I salute the beingness of every individual in that "Movement": whenever any of you make any steps for genuine liberation.

However, recognising that liberation is not simply a matter of law reform (although that may be useful), nor of simple reform of corrupt societal structures (again, although that is probably essential) — and is **never** a matter of violent revolution or forcible overthrow (which always recapitulates the old divisions and concurrent oppressions, although under new labels) — I join with those who realise that true liberation is a matter of **Consciousness Transformation.** Such Consciousness Transformation, however, takes the concerted effort of those who refuse to subcumb to mechanical reactive patterns, who've escaped (to any degree) from the **traps** of the conditioned ego, and have entered the Way of Living required for those who would do the Work of the Ascent of Awareness.

Thus I return to that Aim and Work to which I was called many years ago.

Baraqah bashan!

(The Most Reverend) Bishop Mikhail Itkin, O.D.L.
Metropolitan Bishop
Order of the Divine Love

15 September 1977

FROM *THE GAY ANARCHIST,* SPECIAL ISSUE, 15 SEPTEMBER 1977

ORDER OF THE DIVINE LOVE

Free Christian Community

FROM *ORDER OF THE DIVINE LOVE,* NO DATE, CA. 1977

THE ORDER OF THE DIVINE LOVE is an ecumenical Community for the Harmonious Development of Humanity and the Earth in Christ. As an Order of brothers and sisters who have decicated their lives to the service of all people, by a Way of Living in accord with the Universal Law of Divine Love taught by the Christ in Jesus our Way-Shower, the Work of the Gospel to which we have been called in the Spirit is the Sacramental Work of spiritual renewal, consecration and transformation through the restoration of the ancient Christ-Mysteries for the New Age.

The Prophet says, *Where there is no vision, the people perish (Prov. 29:18);* but to live as people who are both lover and beloved of Life is to live as those who are both lover and beloved of God! Christ says, *I Am come that they might have Life, and that they might have Life more abundant (John 10:10).* In the Creative Spirit of God we are called to bring the Life more abundant to all.

The Work of the Order is that of which the Apostle says, *My little children of whom I travail in birth again, until Christ be formed in you (Gal. 4:19).* Our Work is to enable men and women to discover a new identity, actually our only True Identity--*Christ in us, the hope of glory! (Col. 1:27).* Thus we fulfill the need of Humanity and the Earth for a transforming spirituality in the universal and indwelling Christ, bearing witness at a time of material-technological greatness to the primacy of the spiritual.

> *See, Christ is not outside us, but is innately within us all, but locked up, and in order that Christ may unlock that which is locked up in us, Christ did become outwardly visible. (Amor Proximi)*

We recognise men and women as creative and loving beings, each bearing the Indwelling Light, the Seed of God, the Spark of the Fire of the Divine Love. Thus to become a fully alive, awake and creative person--in accord with the call of the Prophet, *Awake and sing, ye who dwell in dust ...for the Earth shall cast out the dead (Isa. 26:19)*--is to make real in one's Self and to the world the Luminous Image of God within. The Way of Discipleship in the Christ-Truth is the Way of submission to the Will of the One Eternal God--recognising and consciously being a part of the underlying harmony of the vast and beautiful creation of minerals and plants and animals and humans and planets, knowing that All is One in God *in Whom we live and move and have our being (Acts 17:28)* and by Whom we are held in the Unity!

Thus seeking to express our commitment to the One Eternal God, beside Whom there is no other, through the Christ-Truth made known in Jesus: and to be the instruments of the Creative Spirit in the world, we have realised that each of us is required, during our life on Earth, to transform Energies in the Work of reciprocal maintenance. By a Way of Living in accord with the Work of the Christ-Mysteries, we are able to realise Essence: to produce a new quality of Spirit-Beingness. This is the Divine Task given us: To transform Energies by the Way we live our lives!

> *The Christian symbol is a living thing that carries in itself the seed of further development. It can go on developing. It depends only on us, whether we can make up our minds to meditate again, and more thoroughly, on the Christian premise. (C.G. Jung)*

And so it is that this Order comes together to forward the Work of Christ in the world: to bring the Good News to every creature *(Mark 16: 18)* as the Call to make us free *(Luke 4:16-17);* to feed Humanity by the provision for the outpouring of the Divine Love through the teaching of the Word, the administration of the Mysteries (Sacraments) of Light, Love and Liberation, and the performance of the Works of the Divine Love; and thus to encourage the fullest possible development and use of every person's spiritual gifts, talents and ministries, thereby initiating the Work that free persons may do, in the universal and indwelling Christ, to act effectively in the present world-crisis.

In our day, the Order has been called to this Work sometimes known as *Fourth Way Christianity,* which is to say, our Work is not the way of separation from the world--neither that of the Faqir (physical disciplines), nor that of the Monk (emotional disciplines), nor that of the Yogi

FROM *ORDER OF THE DIVINE LOVE,* NO DATE, CA. 1977

(intellectual disciplines). The Fourth Way is the Way of Spiritual Work while remaining in the world but not of it--which integrates and transcends the three ways of separation. It is the *Magnum Opus* for the transformation of Humanity and the World by the actualisation of the Christ in men and women.

By Fourth Way Christianity, the Order recognizes a Way of Living which is not Roman Catholic, Byzantine nor Protestant: nor even a combination of these. Fourth Way Christianity integrates and transcends them ecumenically, by the restoration of the ancient and apostolic Aisor Tradition. Georgi Ivanich Gurdjieff spoke of the Fourth Way as being derived *from a religious order seated near Mount Ararat, the Aisors, a Christian sect tinged with Sufism.*

The ancient Initiates' Vow of the Christ-Mysteries sums up the Work of the Order: *I have beheld a Spark of the Divine in Humanity. That Spark, the universal and indwelling Christ, must be nurtured as the flickering ember is shielded from the driving rain, even at the cost of my life (from the Vows of Profession).* We draw the central inspiration of our Work from an intense faith in the One Eternal God, aside from Whom there is none other: and we know that the universal Christian Community grows in proportion as its members cease to think *solely* in terms of the Christ-Event of two-thousand years ago and strives rather to serve as a vehicle for the Eternal Christ, Who ever guides and sustains Humanity and All Creation: *Before Abraham was, I Am (John 8:58); Wherever two or three are gathered in My Name, there I Am in their midst (Matt. 18:20); Lo, I Am with you always, even unto the consummation of the ages (Matt. 28:20).*

> *That which is called the Christian religion existed among the ancients and never did not exist, from the foundation of the worlds until the Christ came in the flesh, from which time on the same True Religion, which already existed, began to be called Christian. (St. Augustine)*

Being true to our vision of the restoration and renewal of the Apostolic Community of the Pre-Nicene era and to the outpouring of the Spirit in this dawning New Age, we must--with the Gospels--proclaim that the historical Jesus, Son of Mary, became the full embodiment of the Christ-Truth, for which reason our Way-Shower is called Christ Jesus. The same Christ that was in Jesus indwells All-that-is now, and gives the Grace of the One Eternal God for the Work of transformation.

There is Gnosis of God for all Humanity in Christ, Who says: *When you make the two One, when you make the inner as the outer and the outer as the inner and the above as the below, when you make the male and the female into a Single One, so that the male shall not be male and the female not be female, when you make an eye in the place of eyes...then shall you enter the Abode of Truth (Gospel according to St. Thomas: 22).*

During this present day, the Christian religion is called to enter the New Age of the Holy Spirit. A new manifestation of the Androgynous Spirit of the Christ is steadily being unfolded in the thinking, willing and doing of Humanity in the free acceptance of the Deed of Christ. And this is the Way to God: to develop mind, heart and feelings and unite them in harmony with the universal and indwelling Christ, the transcendent Truth at the root of all True Religion.

Gurdjieff wrote of this Work: *The programme of the Institute, the power of the Institute, and the aim of the Institute can be expressed in one sentence: The Institute can help a person to be able to be a Christian.--Simple! That is all!*

Thus it is the purpose of the Order to help prepare the Earth for the New Age that is now dawning--to bring the Illumination of the Christ-Light. This is the Light that Christ promises if we but keep our eye single. It is that Reality that can and must be individually experienced and communally manifested by all who would call themselves Disciples of Christ in the New Heaven and New Earth.

The Work of the Order is undertaken by those who seek to bring into manifestation the Androgynous Spirit of Christ and who have begun to realize that their spirit is condemned to suffocate if it cannot break out of the prison of their operant conditioning and automatically

FROM *ORDER OF THE DIVINE LOVE,* NO DATE, CA. 1977

hardening egotism. Such persons who are ready and able to make long and difficult efforts to establish an effective connection with the Real World, the archetypal-spiritual World, through Work for the Ascent of Awareness in the Christ-Mysteries, are invited to work with this Community.

Love is the Spirit of this Community
and Service is its Work.
And this is our Way:
to live together in Peace,
to seek the Truth in Love,
to help one another in Joy.
(St. Basil, Abbot)

Seeking to be true to that Work, the Order is an ecumenical service and teaching Community, and not a denominational church. However, the Order derives its Work and Teaching from the ancient Christ-Mysteries of the Pre-Nicene Church Catholic, continued in the Aisor Tradition after A.D. 325. We participate in the Aisor Historic Episcopate derived by transmission from the *Syro-Chaldean Evangelical Catholic Communion* within the Oecumenical Apostolic Succession. Thus the Order supplies, to all who have need for them, trained and ordained Priests: sisters and brothers who have dedicated their lives to the service of all Humanity and the Earth in Christ. This is carried out through the agency of the FREE CHRISTIAN COMMUNITY under the Episcopal Oversight of the Order.

Revelation did not cease with the Apostles nor will it cease with any age. God is always greater than our limited understanding, but the Spirit stands ready to reveal the Mysteries of the Divine Love in the universal and indwelling Christ to all who truly seek. Humanity's pathway to unification is a reality, but it is an inner and spiritual one.

Experiencing the need to draw together in community in the Way of Living which the Christ-Mysteries provide in the Work of transformation, we hope to bear witness and convey Blessing to the world as we seek to interpret the importance of the spiritual in practical affaris and common concerns,

that God may be All in all
(I Cor. 15:28).

For further information contact:

ORDER OF THE DIVINE LOVE
7985 Santa Monica Boulevard, Suite 219
West Hollywood, California 90046
Phone: (213) 462-0314 ext 120

FROM *ORDER OF THE DIVINE LOVE,* NO DATE, CA. 1977

The Radical Jesus and Gay Consciousness

Notes for a Theology of Gay Liberation

Bishop Mikhail Itkin

He is among us! Let us celebrate!
And Let Us Be the Instruments of
His Love In this World.

In Memoriam
EDWARD CARPENTER
Prophet of Gay Freedom

****

Author's Introduction to the Second Edition, 1972

The darkness drops again; but now I know
That twenty centuries of stony sleep
Were vexed to nightmare by a rocking cradle,
And what rough beast, its hour come round at last,
Slouches toward Bethlehem to be born?
— *W.B. Yeats, "The Second Coming"*

Requests came in for copies of this monograph and we were out of all copies, when Communiversity West, the experimental college at the California State University at Long Beach agreed to reprint the book. I was faced with a double-bind of major proportions.

Between the first printing of the book and the second, I had been a participant in the "Congress on Religion and the Humanizing of Man" (*sic*) held in Los Angeles by the International Congress of Learned Societies in the Field of Religion. I had taken part in the panel discussions and conversed at length with Radical Feminist theologians (particularly Joan Arnold Pomero, Mary Daly, Rosemary Radford Ruether and the Sisters from W.I.T.C.H. — Women's Inspirational Theological Conspiracy from Harvard) and with some radical male theologians (particularly Thomas J.J. Alizer and William Hamilton, the latter of whom wrote: "My own feeling about the relation of the doctrine of God to the Gay movement is that it is the Christian God itself that is the deepest source of Western persecution of gays, just as I feel, with Norman Mailer that it is that God who is fighting against the Vietnamese people. This God cannot, I think, be redefined, a la Berdyaev or Bonhoeffer, but killed, or set aside, or allowed to die. When this is done, Jesus' call is stripped of its demonic and oppressive power, and becomes liberating.")

Those discussions, further studies in Edward Carpenter's work, and other studies and conversations have all caused tremendous changes in my thinking. If I were writing the monograph today, it would be very, very different. I would particularly like to mention Joan Arnold Romero's seeking for a new symbol for the archetype of God in the Androgynous Community; meetings with the sisters responsible for the book *Women and the World: Toward a Whole Theology* (Graduate Theological Union, Berkeley), conversations with Gay and Church groups about the fundamentalist attacks on the Movement right after the murder attempt at our Hollywood chapel of a young man by some so-called "Jesus People," discussions with Eugene Monick, Minister of the Protestant Episcopal Church and Vicar of St. Clement's in New York City, with German theologian Dorothy Soelle, and with Jim Kepner of ONE, Inc.; feedback from ONE Institute of Homophile Studies where I presented the paper as a lecture; and last but certainly not least, discussions with my teacher Thane Walker, Dean of the Prosperos.

With the prospect of reprinting the book arose, I was confronted with having to decide whether to reprint at all, and if so, whether to rewrite the book thoroughly. I decided against that, particularly in feeling (along with Patricia Wilson of the University of Iowa, with whom on this point I am fully in agreement) that theology today must be *ad hoc*: we can no longer pretend to have the divine Word revealed to us on stone tablets by a patriarchal God out there, but that our construct field must be continually growing, and therefore, our image of divinity must be continually evolving if it is to conform to ontological Truth as we perceive it.

Therefore, I decided to let the paper stand as originally printed, and simply include a brief Preface stating, as clearly as possible *for the moment*, and in a fully *ad hoc* way, my present theological position and suggesting the prospects for further clarification that I see in this field.

****

Author's Preface

> It is not Christianity but our conception and interpretation of it that has become antiquated. The Christian symbol is a living thing that carries in itself the seeds of further development. It can go on developing. It depends only on us whether we can make up our minds to meditate again, and more thoroughly, on the Christian premise.

So writes Carl Gustav Jung. In the ancient Mysteries which antedated Christianity and which provided its background, much was taught about God and about the person's relationship to the Divine. As St. Augustine admitted,

> The true religion was known among the ancients and existed even from the foundation of the world; until the coming of Christ in the flesh, from which time on, that same true religion was called Christian.

Our knowledge of these ancient Mysteries is fragmentary, but we know that in some of the Mystery Schools, when the candidate for the higher Mysteries was given the final degree after many trials and struggles, he/she was told that he/she would be taken into the Presence of God. The candidate was then led to or placed in an empty room where there was nothing and nobody but him/herself. Thus by Initiation was shown the fact of indwelling Divinity — that God must be found within.

Edward Carpenter writes of this:

> Ultimately Humanity will emerge free. We will realize the inner meaning of the creeds and rituals of the ancient religions, and will hail with joy the fulfilment of their far prophecy down the ages — finding after all the long-expected Saviour of the world within our own breast, and Paradise in the disclosure there of the everlasting peace of the soul.

At the International Theology Congress referred to in my Introduction, the sisters from W.I.T.C.H. operated under the ontological statement, "The Universe resounds with the joyous cry, I AM." Again, C.G. Jung wrote,

> We must sooner or later face the question: Are we to understand the "imitation of Christ" in the sense that we should copy his life and, if I may use the expression, ape his stigmata; or in the deeper sense that we are to live our own

> proper lives as truly as he lived his in its individual uniqueness? It is no easy matter to live a life that is modelled on Christ's, but it is unspeakably harder to live one's own life as truly as Christ lived his.

Forms change; life continues, growing, expanding, shaping new forms to match its needs. In order to fulfill our responsibilities we must awaken the Divine potential within: for ourselves, for those in the communities we live and work with, for brothers and sisters we have never seen, for generations yet unborn. This Truth has been elaborated again and again by the Way-Showers and Founders of all the world-religions.

Stripped of excrescences and embellishments, the religions of the world (all of which were founded on Mystery Schools for the awakening of Divinity within, our True Identity, the Indwelling Christ, Ground of Being, Creative Life), all of them, were religions of Love. Particularly, this is true of the Teaching given by Jesus our Brother, Way-Shower and Master Teacher. The highest to which men's and women's minds are turned in a true *metanoia* (turning-again, often mistranslated "repentance") is Truth, Life, Principle. Modern people need, therefore, to experience within reverence for the Life Divine in All and obedience to spiritual Principle in ever increasing Conscious Knowledge of Being, thus bringing into manifestation the Creative Life.

To live as a lover of Life is to live as a lover of the Divine and of all created being possessing the Divine Nature. That which has process of kenotic and dialectic evolution from a primordial simplicity through continuing complexification toward an entirely new coincidence or at-one-ment. The Original Totality (for that which is created in God by God is continuous with God; for God is Being in Itself) or God as the primordial and simple Whole of Reality denied himself by creative fall into evolution. The Transcendent God remains Androgynous Principle, pure Beingness, Beingness being Itself.

This God appears with evolution's initiation, rather than

being a presupposition of creation: since in creation there is Being, or else there would be no creation, this is continuous with God, and that which is continuous with God is God coming into Conscious Knowledge of its true Self. Therefore, we must reject the idea of a "transcendent God alone in eternity" and the concept of *creatio ex nihilo.* The whole of reality, God included, is evolving and the entire course of its history has been a process of Incarnation, because a new kind of coincidence or Identity is being reached. That true Identity is the Christ indwelling all creation and being born anew in manifestation as we become Conscious of the Creative Life-truth-Spirit.

Thus far, this sounds like much that is taught by modern metaphysical movements. However, what is being spoken of is a Christian ontology that goes beyond metaphysical practice and belief as much as that goes beyond the dogmatisms of orthodox christendom. This provides a basis for the renewal — or perhaps for the discovery — in our lives of the Christ-Mystery.

I must make it clear that I am not separating the Christ and Jesus as do most metaphysical teachers and schools, for I fully acknowledge that he who was the historical Jesus of Nazareth became the full embodiment and manifestation of the archetypal and androgynous Christ, which earned for him (and for our benefit, if we can separate this Truth from the veils cast over it by dogmatic Christendom) the title Christ Jesus. For in the evolutionary Incarnation, God continues to empty himself and becomes identified with humanity. This process reaches a focal point and conscious stage in Jesus: God became Jesus to the decisive extent that he died to his otherness in Jesus' life and death. Resurrection and the sending of the Spirit then means that what Jesus became (the total expression of God, the incarnate Word) continues in men and women universally (in *all* humanity) and completely, since the Word exists in no other way except incarnate.

On-goingly one with us in our every now, the incarnate Word, Spirit, Indwelling Christ, brings us progressively closer to a final God/Human androgynous identity. The name of

Jesus our Brother as Liberator, therefore, is not simply to be identified with the historical Jesus, but is used as a symbol of the innermost and highest Reality: the present and continuing unification of the Divine and the Human. In the historic incarnation of Jesus of Nazareth there is shown forth, in the world of space and time, the eternal Process, the eternal sacrifice by which the world is nourished and sustained, proclaimed by the Bible as "the Lamb slain from the foundation of the world" (Rev. 13:8) We manifest this same process of the Creative Life by the sacrifice of our egoistic lower-self to the Higher Self, the Christ, true Being, which is that androgynous Word of which St. John wrote, "...was in the beginning with God...All things were made by the Word; and without that Word was not anything made that was made. In the Word was Life; and the Life was the Light of all people." (John 1: 1–4)

The final identity or *coincidentia oppositorum* is a fully dialectical one. It stands at the furtherest dialectical remove from either God as the Original Totality or God as other than human. It is not a mere juxtaposition or harmony of Divinity and Humanity, nor even a close unity in which the opposites somehow retain their own identities: but if we follow the desire for the Creative Life when it arises in us, it will lead to the birth of Christ consciously as our true Being. In this sense, the Christ is not the property of any religion, but the symbol of Universal Life.

Thus God and humanity cease to be what they were as separated. They become a new Identity. While in the past God, as separate, was psychically — and therefore, theologically — real, that God has really died to this separateness in the process of evolutionary Incarnation (cf. Phil. 2: 5–11). By this evolution, humanity also is radically different than what we used to be — so different that we can no longer, in any way, depend on a God separate from ourselves. We can, indeed, no longer even realistically conceive of such a God. In a sense, God is still alive: *but not as separate from humanity, from living men and women, from the cosmos.*

Martin Buber writes:

> Man wishes to be confirmed in his being by man, and wishes to have a presence in the being of the other. The human person needs confirmation because man as man needs it. Sent forth from the natural domain of the species into the hazard of the solitary category, surrounded by the air of a chaos which came into being with him, secretly and bashfully he watches for a Yes which allows him to be and which can come to him only from one human person to another. It is from one man to another that the heavenly bread of Self-being is passed.

But before we can pass that heavenly bread to one another, we must experience the Creative Life, the Indwelling Christ, incarnate in the depths of our Being. The incarnation of the Christ as the Creative Life within us and amongst us is the birth of a new Consciousness. When the Master-Teacher spoke of the Realized Kingdom, the androgynous Community of Love, the Aramaic word that he deliberately chose signified both that "the kingdom of God is *within* you" and "the kingdom of God is *amongst* you." (Luke 17:21)

Thus it is apparent that Christianity, to be true to its transforming capacity, must be completely contemporary (or "non-religious" to use Bonhoeffer's phrase), i.e. it must reject every retreat into the past and any effort to devalue humanity — personally or collectively — and the world. All such maneuvers are betrayals of the Incarnation: which is the specific difference of Christianity's Teaching from that of religions. Traditional Christendom, however, is "religious" in precisely this sense: in that it tries to resist this incarnational evolution toward Divine/Human and Androgynous Identity by resurrecting Jesus as a cosmic Lord. Churches have tried to conceal the realization of the Oneness of the Divine/Human, Male/Female polarities, by their positing of Jesus as an extra-terrestrial cosmic Lord. This negates humanity's real present and future, returning to the dead past by trying to cling to the image of a separate and eternal God, by closing off revelation with the Apostolic times and by claiming that faith remains unchanged and autonomous, despite the changing world.

Some Gay Liberationists postulate the meaning of Gay male liberation as being "the freeing of the sister in us." Women theologians put forth the ontological Truth: "The Universe resounds with the joyous cry — I Am!" We are today living in that Third Age prophesied by Joachim of Fiore in the Fifteenth Century: an apocalyptic time of the death of God — one as different from the New Testament as the New Testament is from the Old Testament. Scripture no longer can be considered a closed revelation, but merely as a pointer to inner Truth, to be validated or discarded on the basis of inner experience. The images of a "transcendent God" and a "cosmic Christ" are increasingly empty and dead, precisely in as much as the only real Word of revelation and faith is incarnate in men and women and steadily approaching the full apocalyptic identity of God and Humanity.

The Body of Christ, therefore, is the entire world. We may perhaps even be bold enough to say that the Word is even more present and active outside the churches than within them because of their "religious" nature. However, since *all* of Reality is a process of Incarnation by which "the Great Humanity Divine" arises, we should not retreat from the process nor obstruct the goal but should give ourselves completely to the evolving actuality or our present which is the incarnate Word.

****

The above *ad hoc* statement of where I now stand, ontologically and theologically, will cast the following monograph in a different light than it was in when written.

C. G. Jung writes: "I have often made mistakes and have often had to wipe the slate clean of previous knowledge in order to acquire what is most pertinent." If I were writing the monograph today, I would put more attention to the development of that Gay consciousness which is the result of individuation, of the personal realization of the androgynous Divine/Human nature of the Self and Its manifestation in community. I would put less emphasis on the degrees of Gay oppression, a story that has been told often, and which is no less true now, but which does not require the constant retelling. I would put less emphasis on the oppressive nature of institutional churches, following the admonition to "Let the dead bury their dead" (Matt. 8:22): and instead strive to develop the positive ways towards a liberated consciousness for a liberated society.

Finally, if I were rewriting the monograph today, I would very likely withdraw the closing Meditation on the Lord's Prayer to consider it for re-writing. Therefore, in place of that or, more realistically, in addition to that, I would like to offer this:

The Christian mythos provides a transforming meditation of the mind, heart and feelings: a creative encounter with the eternal Self:

> Turning inward, letting go of all outer concerns of the personal ego,
> I seek that Center which is the Christ within—the Self that is One with the Self in all.
> From that Center, I—the eternal Self—perceive all manifestations of the Creative Life, all forms incarnating Divinity, each revealing even as it seems to conceal the form of beauty.
> From that Center, I realize the Unity of All Life.
> From that Center, I hear the magnificent symphony of Life's harmonious unfolding.
> From that Center, I see all things made new.
> From that Center, I make all things new.
> I am one with Light. Now I say in the words of the ancient prayer:
> "O Christ, Thou Word of God
> My own Eternal Self,

Live Thou Thy Life in me;
Do Thou Thy Will in me;
Be Thou Made Flesh in me;
I have no will but Thine,
I have no self but Thee."*

The Universe resounds with the joyous cry:
I Am.
Now from that Self Immortal, I return, inwardly reharmonized, taking up again the tasks of my days, the personal self renewed in the Light of the Christ within.
Thus I resolve to move ever Self-recollected, ever in the Self of the Christ in whom I live and move and have my Being;** sharing with each I meet the heavenly bread of Self-being that all persons may know the Self eternal, the Self that is One with All.
And so it is.

Dr. Michael-Francis Itkin
(Bishop Mikhail)
Los Angeles, California
14.x.72 B 2122 hours

* words of an ancient Celtic prayer
**Acts 17:28 adapted

Preface to the Second Edition printed by: The Community of the Creative Life and Quest Institute Free Christian Communion (United Episcopal) for insertion in the monograph printed by: Communiversity West B Experimental College, California State University at Long Beach.

– I –
NOTES FOR A THEOLOGY OF GAY LIBERATION

> "The Cross awaits not only the individual person, but also society as a whole, the State or a civilization. In its application to social life the Cross does not imply an acceptance of social conditions, but rather an acceptance of the idea of inevitable revolution and radical social change. It is a profound error to regard the Cross in a conservative light." — *Nicolai Berdyaev*

> "We are a menace to you, O civilization!
> We have seen you — we allow you —
> we bear with you for a time,
> But beware! For in a moment and,
> when the hour comes, inevitably,
> We shall arise and sweep you away!"
> — *Edward Carpenter*

Whenever a people begin to transcend the kinds of identities which are imposed upon them by their social environment and begin to assert a self-defined identity, they become the expression of a fundamental spiritual reality which is part of all humanity. Gay Liberation, as it has come to exist, is not an organized or monolithic thing. Arising in response to long felt needs, it consists of many small groups and individuals to whom the life thus far forced upon them is far more to be feared than the penalties to be faced by being open about homosexuality. Its membership cuts across many class and political lines, previously defined, to assume only one clear line of demarcation: the afraid and the unafraid — or, more accurately, those who can live with their fear, and not be overcome by it, and those who cannot.

Gay people today are learning that nobody gives you freedom. It is something you have to demand and insist upon! Whether this is just or not is a good question: but every minority group and oppressed people has to face the reality of it.

What, then, does it mean to speak of our oppression and our liberation as Gay people?

Oppression is a reality, both social and psychological, affecting all of us in varying degrees, outwardly economically, legally and socially, and inwardly in our physical, emotional and intellectual centers: inhibiting our lives, causing us to be less than we are capable of being. Gay oppression is a *systematic* process which derives from the narrow roles of our anti-sex and anti-life society: roles which we have internalized.

The question of Gay oppression, however, cannot be divorced from the many-faceted questions of human sexuality in general and the oppression of other minority groups; it must be seen in relation to the oppression of men and women forced into socio-sexual role playing. We must, however, remember that even while we are striving to analyze our oppression we must continue the social struggle for our liberation. Intellectual analysis is not enough; and the only viable analysis able to affect true physical, emotional and intellectual freedom will grow from the struggle itself, both socially and inwardly.

We are a minority people struggling to create our own subculture. No other minority group, so far as I know, has had that problem. In the process, it is necessary to take note of all the various aspects of our reality and give them expression. The immediate issue is that we must continue and intensify the struggle for Gay Freedom — and thus create a new Gay Consciousness.

The Sources of Gay Oppression

In this light, we must proceed to the question as to what the source and forms of Gay oppression are. (I must point out that I write this as a Gay male, and I can not claim to be speaking to the question of the double oppression faced by my Lesbian sisters.)

The dominant culture in our society is anti-sexual as a whole, and anti-Gay in particular. As Gay men we are oppressed by limitations on sensuality and compassion. There is an abridgement of our freedom to determine our sexuality in accord with our deepest urges and to be expressive with other men. We have been taught to fear our sensuality. Sex-role separation, the denial of the feminine within us, the demand to live up to the macho/stud/All-American image, make us unable to be whole and to realize all aspects of ourselves. We are divided from our sisters by sexuality and from our brothers by competition, since male competitiveness is seen in our society as desirable and therefore stimulated and even forced upon us from early childhood in competitive sports. We are, in a very real sense, traitors to the roles males are expected to play in this society, in that each male is expected to keep at least one woman in subjugation as a wife and, if he can afford it, more than one as mistresses; and by virtue of our being Gay, we betray this role and invite the vengeance of society.

We are oppressed by the definition of certain essential human traits as "feminine and weak" and therefore "undesirable." From the fear of rejection for this "weakness," we come to fear love: this denial of our androgynous nature being the source of machismo, of sham strength. Our sex-role identification often leads to either an over-intensification of the macho image, or to its total rejection leading in turn to a greater rejection of the person by Society, which is internalized in forms of self-hatred.

We are oppressed by our inability to express our fears. We are supposed to be always dominant, and if we cannot "master" that in an aggressive way, we recede into ourselves.

In Western society, *the nuclear family* is the institution most people encounter, and it has the greatest effect in forming personalities. We are treated as objects or possessions by our parents, never granted our personhood, subject to an authoritarian upbringing that generates internalized guilt and resentment ("do this, do that; stop this, it's naughty") and cripples our ability to accept criticism, to grow and to change.

The family is where sexual response is learned, where children are subjected daily to the separation of the physical and the sensual. Male children are encouraged to be physical and athletic, but not sensitive or sensual. This prevents integrated lives and results in the brutalization of the physical, and Gay men, who find such brutal physicality as rough-housing, competitive sports and warfare repugnant and avoid them, are forced by the ideological hegemony of sex-roles, begun in the nuclear family, to internalize societal rejection as inadequacy. Sexism — oppression of and discrimination against persons because of sex or sexuality, and the treatment of persons as objects — begins right here.

The educational system reinforces the anti-sexual and anti-Gay attitudes learned in the family. In a society where labor, schooling, art and sexual relations are expressions of alienation, we are oppressed by individualistic isolation.

It is only through collective vulnerability that we can truly build personal strength; but the educational system, with its competitive grading, makes such collectivity next to impossible and perpetuates, instead, the mass-consumer society where each competes to own more things (including, as possessions, depersonalized women).

We are oppressed by the lack of non-alienating outlets for self-expression in the educational process. We are oppressed by being denied the knowledge of Gay people in history, by the orientation of all education towards monolithic history. We are denied not only the knowledge of our own Gay history, but knowledge of the history of others who resisted this sexist and racist system. Homosexuality, when discussed in the schools, receives heavy negative sanctions both directly and by treating it in lurid, joking ways.

Since the educational system imprisons us from very early childhood through at least late adolescence and, increasingly, through early adulthood, the impact of that system is considerable and second only to that of the nuclear family.

Thomas Merton wrote:

> We are living in a society that's absolutely sick — and one of the reasons why it's sick is that it's completely from the top of the head. It's completely cerebral. It has utterly neglected the rest of the man; the whole human person is reduced to a very small part of who and what he is...And Christianity has connived with this. *Official Christianity* has gone along with this kind of repressive & partial & fragmented view of man, and now we have to face the consequences.

The oppression of Gay people and anti-sexual repression in general stems almost entirely from *institutional religion* in the Judaeo-Christian culture: what Merton calls "official Christianity." This is not to say that it finds any basis in the revolutionary Teaching of transforming Love which Jesus brought to us. However, modern civilization, founded on the dogmatic structures of the institutional Church (even where it has been largely rejected on conscious levels) has since 325 C.E. followed in the anti-life, anti-sex teachings of Paul rather than in the liberating Way of Jesus.

The institutional Church's original misrepresentations of the Love-ethic of Jesus was rooted in the anti-sexual attitudes of Paul and the Church Fathers. This early anti-sexuality has been perpetuated for 1800 years as a power-play by the institution and has embittered the lives of its victims for approximately ninety generations. In the wake of the bloody Crusades, the "witch-" and "faggot-" burnings of the Middle Ages and Salem, and the Inquisition, the churches of Christendom provide the philosophical-moral undergirding for the sexism, male chauvinism and anti-homosexuality taught in the homes and schools, even as they continue blessing racist and imperialist wars.

All of the legal sanctions against Gay people find their origin in the dogmatic traditions of Christendom. The Church has been guilty of what is, at the least, a gross insensitivity to the sexual needs of living human beings — adults, adolescents and children. The separation of body and spirit, the cut-off from essential feelings and the alienation from Self all trace their origins to the teaching of the institutional Church and for untold numbers of people, sexual freedom and personhood are still sacrificed to the restrictions imposed by the Constantinian Church's power elite.

In spite of which, there is a liberating core to the Christian mythos which can provide spiritual strength for the struggle for Gay Liberation and the liberation of all peoples. As Jeff McIntyre wrote in *Blood of the Lamb,* the student magazine of Chicago's McCormack Theological Seminary:

> Jesus Christ was a revolutionary.... He exemplifies the revolutionary life. He didn't fuck around with the technocrats and bureaucrats and fat cats of his day. He told them all where they could go. Christ was hung on the cross. It is a historical fact that to be hung on the cross in those days you had to be a political prisoner, an enemy of the state. For one thing, I'm sick and tired of all this theologizing about revolution that has been coming down from a lot of liberal types who haven't got anything better to do with their time.... We keep hearing about the theology of hope. Some dude has written a whole big book about it. Well, the theology of hope is when you've done all the organizing you can for the liberation of the oppressed people of the earth and you've got forty kinds of F.B.I. agents and other local pigs on your neck and you just stand there and say fuck off, just like Christ did for the court.

There *are* injustices: police brutality, entrapment, employment and housing discrimination, laws. It's not enough now to speak of morality, to urge us to carry our crosses as the churches have been doing for centuries. We are Gay Christians, free brothers and sisters who stand proud in the strength of Jesus' resurrection with all that makes us what we are. And we now demand that His Church call out from the rooftops for justice and freedom, to brave the opposition of an unloving world and refashion social thinking.

The Church has to be blamed for much of our suffering. Nonetheless, sincere Gays turn to that same Church, hoping desperately to find the face of Jesus, to hear His voice, to feel His hand. The Church must share blame and so has responsibility to undo the resultant social injustices.

Gay Christians are ready enough to add our voices to the thunderous cry of blame hurled at the Church. Yet we must share a part of it. What have *we* done to alleviate our condition? Too many are content to live as homosexuals with tortured conscience, to walk away from it all and curse, to refuse to fight for our heritage, to refuse to stand up for justice. Many homosexual Christians have not faced up to their own Gayness, have not accepted it, have no pride in it. Their own lethargy, their own cowardice, have allowed the injustices to multiply and become established.

It is time now to come out of the closet, to quit running, to take a stand and fight with whatever time and talent are possible. It is time to recover our heritage and be proud. Yes, the Church bears a very great part of the blame for the plight of Gays; but if the Church has a responsibility to correct injustices, so much the more do we Gay people ourselves have the responsibility to speak up and work for our freedom.

However, the deepest problem faced by Gay people in our personal lives is that of positive self-image. *The psychiatric establishment* which has set itself up as the authority, puts forth theories which cause Gay people to view themselves as inferior and sick with categories of "deviant, abnormal, infantile," etc. Establishment psychiatric thought tends to think of sexuality in purely genital terms and thus reinforces sexual role-playing by its definition of heterosexual coitus as the only truly "mature" sexual act and dismissal of all other acts as "immature" or merely as "sexual foreplay." Psychiatry thus sets up a negative propaganda barrage which leads many homosexuals of both sexes to seek psychiatric "help" to be "cured" of their homosexuality by brutal aversion tortures, shock treatments and other "therapies."

As dogmatic religion has lost some of its overt control of society and culture, its reins have been handed over to the new high priests of dogmatic pseudo-science in the form of medical practitioners.

All levels of *government* exert heavy anti-Gay pressures through laws, police harassment and entrapment, police raids and shootings of Gay people, persecution within the military and in government jobs (setting the standard for private industry), all of which oppress Gay people in concrete, painful and sometimes fatal ways.

Business forces the second-class status of Gay people through anti-Gay hiring practices and unequal opportunities for Gays within the workplace. Gays, when "discovered" at places of employment, are often fired or denied promotion. Open Gays often have difficulty finding adequate housing and in Gay ghetto areas, when housing is available, it is often overpriced and of poor quality. Gays are exploited through over-priced and sexist bars, films, magazines, hustler-model agencies, clothing shops, etc.

We are oppressed by a *consumer society* and the projection of unattainable roles and characteristics by ruling-class sexist and racist *media* (e.g. Marvel Comics heroes, James Bond, the Playboy Man). The media extol and reinforce cultural norms, projecting macho hero images and a negative picture of homosexuality. Mass media magazines, film and TV emphasize identification with stereotyped male chauvinism and a consumer approach to sexuality.

In major cities, the Gay ghetto area is a prime target for exploitation by *organized crime* — the combined force of criminal syndicates and their police allies. The oppressed situation of Gay people and our expected lack of social support or power base makes us easy victims of exploitation in syndicate-owned, police-paid-off bars, baths, pornographic movies, etc. These two criminal elements — the syndicate and the police — exploit our needs for relatively safe places to meet and socialize with other Gay people — which exploitation does not exclude police crackdowns every election year and the ever-present threat of assault and murder.

The oppression of Gay people at the hands of a white, het, male ruling class undergirds and strengthens the State and its authoritarian, bureaucratic structures, using us as scapegoats by raising the cry of "immorality, vice, sickness, aberration, deviation," in an on-going effort to distract public attention from the real and pressing social ills of our time: sexism and racism at home, imperialism abroad, violence against humanity and against the earth. The periodic raids on bars and other Gay meeting places (and, oppressive as the bar scene is, in many places it is all our community has), arrests, dismissals from jobs, black-listings and tortuous "therapies" all constitute a part of the establishment's use of the so-called "homosexual problem" as a veil behind which can be hidden totalitarian attacks on the right to peace, freedom, human dignity and the autonomy of the person.

Towards Liberation

Faced with this oppression, we must struggle against it and out of the struggle itself, develop a new strategy of how to forge a new society. Although we can learn from the analyses of the past, we must acknowledge that they no longer fit the needs of our times.

We are an oppressed people just coming fully into a consciousness of our oppression and just beginning a higher stage in the struggle for our liberation. This puts us in a unique position: and from that place, we can perhaps see a new way for humanity, a way out of the morass, a transcendent society. As Albert Camus said, "From a certain point of view, the meaning of tomorrow's history is not what we think it to be. It is contained in the struggle between creativity and inquisition."

It is perfectly apparent that the old ways do not work. The governments of the world, all of which claim to speak for "freedom" in spite of their differing clich s of capitalism or socialism, are destroying cultures, subjecting all persons to an alienating computer technology, jailing thousands for daring to express their loving sexuality or explore their own consciousness with disapproved substances, and poisoning the very air we breathe and the food we eat, making the planet less inhabitable. In spite of the high-sounding phrases issuing from the cabinets of government and the controlled media, we are not free: we are daily subjected to the most sophisticated public relations campaign on the part of the State and the Military-Commercial-Academic-Ecclesiastical complex (using psychology and the social sciences) which seek to keep us as a manipulative, destructive society.

"Against the ruin of the world," wrote Kenneth Rexroth, "there is only one defense — the creative act." No armed force holds the key to the future. War — violence — is the health of the State: and the State, whenever and wherever it exists, is a potential Buchenwald or Dachau with humans as guinea-pigs (see California's Atascadero State Hospital for a contemporary example). The State is the potential napalming of men, women and children, the destruction of entire civilian villages, genocide rampant. The State is always based on the ability to deliberately condition the mind-set of lynchers and of those who authorized the bombing of Hiroshima and the destruction of My Lai. A revolutionary State is always a betrayal of revolutionaries, whether at Kronstadt or in the Cuban Venceremos brigades or the concentration camps for Gays.

The sole power the State possesses is that psychic energy it has stolen from the individual members of society — by techniques of sexual and emotional repression, by the manipulation of sex-roles through the mass media and the disallowing of the free inner search for human potential. By itself — without this stolen energy — the State is but a legal myth.

In some ways, in spite of our oppression as Gays, we are very fortunate. A very large part of these media campaigns are directed through expected sexual roles. Insofar as we have rejected these roles and freed out heads of guilt over this rejection, we gain insight into both the sexual role-playing and its manipulation by the State. There's a lot that we can teach straights about love and sexuality, and we can help them see though the myths that keep the establishment going.

As Paul Goodman writes,

> Society knows the repressions that make its existence possible, but to the members of Society this knowledge has become unconscious. In this way is achieved the maximum of coercion by the easiest means. Many, I believe most, of the so-called crimes are really free acts whose repression causes our timidity; natural society has a far shorter list of crimes. But, on the contrary, there is now an important class of acts that are really crimes and yet are judged indifferent or with approval by law and morals both. Acts which lead to unconcerned behavior are crimes. The separation of natural concern and institutional behavior is not only the sign of coercion, but is positively destructive of natural societies....The crime that these persons, we all in our degree, are committing happens to be the most heinous in jurispurudence: it is a crime worse than murder. It is Treason. Treason against our natural societies so far as they exist. Not all commit Treason to our natural societies in the same degree; some are more the principals, some more the accomplices. But it is ridiculous to say that the crime can not be imputed or that any one commits it without intent and in ignorance. For every one knows moments in which he conforms against his nature, in which he suppresses his best spontaneous impulse and cowardly takes leave of his heart. The steps which he takes to habituation and unconsciousness are crimes which entail every subsequent evil of en-

> slavement and mess murder.... We see that in fact everybody who still has life and energy is continually manifesting some natural force and is today facing an unnatural coercion. And now, in some apparently trivial issue that nevertheless is the key, he *draws the line!* The next step for him to take is not obscure or difficult, it presents itself at once; it is even forcibly presented by Society! Modern society does not let one be — it is too total — it forces one's hand!

For Gay people the line was drawn when on June 28, 1969, Gays fought back, for the first time, when a Gay bar was raided and brothers and sisters were being arrested. Having once drawn the line, Gay Pride was born at the Stonewall in New York City; the Gay Freedom Movement was born, and we cannot go back.

The struggle of Gay people for freedom has four general aspects:

1) the attempt to talk to homosexuals, to get them to accept themselves and to accept others like them as people;

2) the effort to tear down the ghetto — mental as well as physical — and its exploitative agencies, to oppose heterosexual role-playing, the internalization of stereotypes; the challenging of personally B and socially B destructive behavior patterns, sex as non-encounter instead of human encounter, and so on;

3) the attack on the oppression from society, which comes upon us in many subtle and unsubtle ways, many of which were described above; and

4) the building of a positive Gay alternative culture through the service of our people in day-to-day needs, the recovery of Gay history and heritage, and the discovery of a creative Gay consciousness.

The Gay Freedom Movement exists to carry on the struggle in these areas.

The struggle against sexism, the struggle for Gay freedom, is truly revolutionary: for with the coming of Women's and Gay freedom, all of the racist and imperialist myths must also fall. (Shulamith Firestones's *The Dialectic of Sex* should be read in this regard.) However, we cannot achieve this under a system of over-production of goods and under-distribution to the starving peoples of the world. We cannot achieve our freedom under either a capitalist system nor, as has been shown by recent history, under a bureaucratic centralist or State-"socialist" system. A true socialism must be based upon an end to the competitive nature of society; and thus so-called "socialist" states that oppress Women and Gay men, and foster international competition, are not truly Socialist.

A true socialism can only be built upon the basis of Women's and Gay freedom, which, by their overthrow of all competitive sexual and social models, will bring about the end of all bureaucracy and capitalism. Such a true socialism will come forth from the integral realization of the Self actualized in Community, the restoration of the unity of body and spirit.

Dogmatic Christendom has spoken so strongly and so long of the separation of body and spirit, and repressed the body and the material, brutally in many instances, in favor of the development of a cerebralized "spiritual" that we are now at that impasse of which Thomas Merton wrote. At the same time, much of that which has called itself revolutionary has denied the Spirit and its values, and thus produced a lifeless art and culture, a static and anti-life society.

The true revolutionary urge is an integrated and creative urge, combining body and spirit, contemplation and action, into one in the here-and-now moment. Thus Judith Malina and Julian Beck of the Living Theatre wrote:

> In the secret quarter, in the underground, in Greenwich Village and Saint Germain, among

> the campus students planning sit-ins and freedom rides, wherever change is sought, in the midst of changes, in the march to the sea, in the picket lines in front of embassies, the worth of the world is proclaimed. In the invisible lofts where the anarchists and pacifists defy money and the structure of society, where the lies are being examined and reversed, lies which are the allies of death, in these places is the poetry which is the language of God.

The true revolution is that which Gary Snyder describes as

> a continuing revolution of consciousness, which will be won not by guns but by seizing the key images, myths, archetypes, eschatologies and ecstasies so that life won't seem worth living unless one's on the transforming energies' side.

Smash the Closets Down

screaming lavender echo —
hunger...
hunger...
hunger
beneath echo
young boy/young girl
hiding in closet
stares through black mirror
toying with smile.
Human manifestation of the holy
hidden in shadows
pronouncing silent words —

hunger...
hunger...
hunger
nothing!
No response -
love dies beneath cup of emptiness
pierced by flaming sword
and there returns to self.
Requiem in silence —
hunger...
hunger...
hunger.
Faceless boy/girl of all the faces,
faces of 6000 years of hiding -
now,
gently.
touch your sex
and in arousal
no longer hide your eyes,
velvet deep within liquid dreams.
whose are the others —
staring —
the little eyes of little people
shut in rejecting oncoming light!
"the word become flesh!" —
you must become known
that *we* shall be free!
Smash the closets down,
tear the walls down,
burn the barriers down,
end the cry of hunger...
hunger...
hunger

A Radical Gay Christian Vision

For those of us in the Western world whose psychic roots are firmly planted in Judaeo-Christian soil, this revolution which comes from total integration into the process of Life can best be achieved through a radical transformation of the Christian mythos.

> I would like your energy:
> among a thousand winds
> your Body is of this world!
> This is your Spirit among us:
> psychic fire-fingers play
> across my spine,
> my centers of nerve and energy.
> Brother Jesus,
> You & I have wrestled
> naked in the city streets.
> You are Love, Brother Flesh,
> Brother Jesus,
> Messiah & Liberator,
> You are Love!

As Brazilian theologian, Ruben Alves, writes:

> The creation of history is possible only through power. But the use of power is politics. The new humanity and the new tomorrow are to be shaped in and through an activity which is political in character. Politics is no longer regarded as the activity of a few, the play of power among elites. It is the vocation of humanity, because every person is called to participate, in one way or another, in the creation of the future.

Carl Gustav Jung wrote:

> I am convinced that it is not Christianity but our conception and interpretation of it that has become antiquated. The Christian symbol is a living thing that carries in itself the needs of further development. It can go on developing. It depends only on us whether we can make up our minds to meditate again, and more thoroughly, on the Christian promise.

Likewise, the World Council of Churches, in its meeting at New Delhi, India in November 1961 declared that

> Many, within and without the Christian Church, are puzzled about the relationship between God, man and nature. There is urgent need for the development of a theology of nature, as part of an inclusive theology, and its statement in language that can be understood by the man in the pew or the laboratory.

There is, in the same manner, an urgent need for the development of a theology of liberation, and specifically of Gay Liberation.

In seeking for such a radical transformation of the Christian premise, we must labor with all our energy in behalf of a new theology: one not based on the old and tired concept of the "fall of man" with all people inheriting "original sin" with the resultant necessity of still being redeemed in spite of the Incarnation; rather, a theology based on the ascent of humanity with all being confronted with the challenge and opportunity to grasp and use all the resources before them, including the fruit of the tree of knowledge, with the resultant purpose of life being to grow, to grow toward realization of the Divine, to grow toward ever higher manifestation of life — in which evolution becomes the greatest story of life in Jesus ever told.

As the philosopher Nicholai Berdyaev put it,

> It seems as though the church had never fully recognized that in Christ and through Christ, man is already a new creature, that in him new power and freedom are manifest. After Christ, original sin no longer has absolute power over man; man and the cosmos no longer belong to the natural order; the break between the natural and the supernatural has been overcome; spiritual life, spiritual creativeness, may now be manifested in the world and in man.

Part of the radical transformation of the Christian mythos was pointed to by the theologian Dietrich Bonhoeffer, who spoke of God being edged out of the world, now that the world has come of age:

> And the only way to be honest is to recognize that we have to live in the world as it God did not exist. And this is just what we do see— before God. So our coming of age forces us to a true recognition of our situation with God. God is teaching us that we must live as men who can get along very well without him.... The God who makes us live in this world without using him as a working hypothesis is the God before whom we are ever standing. God allows himself to be edged out of the world and onto the cross. God is weak and powerless in the world, and that is exactly the way, the only way, in which he can be with us and help us.

Human religiosity has caused us to look in our distress to the power of God in the world; looking to God as someone who can miraculously pull us out of trouble. For too long we have cried: "God, we believe; we have told You we believe. We have not denied You, then rise up and defend us. Acknowledge us, oh God, before the whole world. Give us also the right to our existence." (Radclyffe Hall, *The Well of Loneliness*). This cry of Gay people has echoed through the ages.

Now, however, we are called in Jesus to take up the struggle for our own libertion: the Bible directs us to the powerlessness and suffering of God who emptied himself of all triumph, power and lordship to become the Suffering Servant of all, to die for us on the Cross of Golgotha and to rise for us as the Spirit of Jesus present and within all humanity.

The process by which the world came of age was an abandonment of a false conception of God, and a clearing of the decks for the God of the Bible, who became one with humanity in Jesus and who conquers power and space in the world by his weakness.

The Way of Jesus in Bonhoeffer's radical secularization does not, in any way, rule out a life which is lived in a secret discipline of prayer and meditation, study, worship and silence even while being engaged in the struggles of the oppressed. Behind these two elements and uniting them is the unshaken certitude that faith is not something the individual person dreams up and consequently has to nurture and defend against attack, but rather the result of existential confrontation with the Presence of Jesus in the world, in humanity, in the "Thou" of other persons, an initiative which comes from "the other side" to us, with its own inexplicable and inescapable reality.

As Dionysius the Areopagite put it:

> He who is the pre-eminent Cause of all things sensibly and intelligently perceived, is not himself any of those things; nor can any affirmation or negation be applied to him, for although we may affirm or deny the things below him, we can neither affirm or deny him, inasmuch as the all-perfect and unique Cause of all things transcends all affirmation, and the simple preeminence of his absolute nature is outside of every negation — free from every limitation and beyond them all.

Likewise, as Paul Tillich says:

> The name of this infinite and inexhaustible depth and ground of all being is God. That depth is what the word God means. And if that word has not much meaning for you, translate it, and speak of the depths of your life, of the source of your being, of your ultimate concern, of what you take seriously without any reservation. Perhaps, in order to do so, you must forget everything traditional that you have learned about God. Perhaps even the word itself. For if you know that God means depth, you know much about him. You cannot then call yourself an atheist or unbeliever. For you cannot think or say: Life has no depth! Life is shallow. Being itself is surface only. If you could say this in complete seriousness you would be an atheist; but otherwise you would not.

The Good News is that if Jesus could realize his identity with God, we can also — but this God can not be idolized as an imperious monarch with a royal court or ministering angels. God, as the "depth and ground of all being," the love which moves the sun and other stars, is something much more inward, intimate and mysterious — in the sense of being too close to be objectivised but always to remain the "Thou" of "I-Thou" dialogue, in community and inwardly, as Presence for us in Jesus our Brother.

Following in Bonhoeffer's footsteps, Alec Lea, an English Quaker, has suggested a change in our vocabulary. He says that we should eliminate the word "almighty" in reference to God:

> The purpose of a God of love must be to overcome evil by good and if this is not the purpose of Christianity then Jesus lived and died in

> vain. To overcome evil with superior power could only be the purpose of a god of power. We betray ourselves... by clinging to a conception of God which is pre-Christian, which is, at best, an uneasy mixture of love and power needing to be continually shaken up, like oil and water. From this mixture we can extract all the power and yet find that which is left is still divine. But what do we have left when we extract all the love? Perhaps the time has come to apply Acton's famous dictum about power to Almighty God and so dethrone him in favor of Unmighty God, the vulnerable spirit of love which, like water, is essentially soft and yielding, but by persistence overcomes everything in the end.
>
> Looking inwards, we find God and simultaneously we find weakness. Let us accept our divine weakness and call it non-violence. Since there never was and never will be anything divine about power, we must learn at long last *not* to say "Almighty God."[1]
>
> To sum up, God is always the soft answer that turns away wrath, never the thunderbolt of righteous anger. The wages of sin is never death, but always sorrow and pity.

In like manner, the Eastern Orthodox philosopher-theologian Nicolai Berdyaev, writes:

> In relation to the world God is freedom, rather than necessity and determination. But when we speak of freedom we speak of the supreme mystery. Men have made God into a determining cause, into power and might, just as they have made him lord and tsar. But He resembles none of these: He is quite beyond the limits of such

> categories. In a certain sense God has less power than a policeman, a soldier or a banker. And we must stop speaking of God and His providence as we speak of the governing of states in this world. This is all a false objectification....
>
> The base human category of lordship is not applicable to God, God is not the lord and He does not lord it over men. No authority is inherent in God, He has no will to power; He does not demand the slavish worship of a bond-servant. God is freedom; He is the liberator, not the master. God gives a sense of liberty, not of subjection. God is spirit, and spirit knowns no such relationship as that of master and slave.... God can act freely, only in freedom and by means of freedom....
>
> The God of revelation, the God of the Bible is not the Absolute: in Him there is dramatic movement and life, relationship to another, to man and the world...God is not an absolute monarch: He is a God who suffers with the world and with man; He is crucified Love, the Liberator. And the Liberator appeared, not as authority, but as crucifixion. The Redeemer is the Liberator, not the accounting with God for crimes committed. God reveals himself as Human-ness. Human-ness is the chief quality of God, not at all omnipotence, omniscience, etc., but humaneness, freedom, love, sacrifice. The concept of God must be freed from distorting, degrading, profane sociomorphism.

In this meditation on the Christian premise which we are undertaking, this seeking for a radical transfiguration of the Christian mythos that Dr. Jung and the World Council of Churches call for, we must look first to the Gospel Faith of transforming Love as lived by the apostolic and primitive

Church community, the first disciples of Jesus, and recorded in the Bible and other contemporaneous documents. As Bishop James Pike said,

> *The Dead Sea Scrolls* and other finds have opened the door to a wealth of new insights. But perhaps the most significant aspect of the study for Church alumni is the primitive religious outlook that continually reasserted itself against the fixities, indeed idolatries, of the agricultural and town, or city, mode of life. The origins of Christianity were infused with the spirit of the desert, the nomadic life of the wilderness: God on the move with his people, no finality other than God, no "temples made with hands." In contrast to the organization of Christian denominations in our day, of which the basic unit is the parish (a settled congregation with a building or buildings designed to serve a particular geographical area and thus suitable to an agricultural mode of life), the nomad religion that was the heart of our origins is far more suitable for today's post-rural, post-urban people for whom the city never really became home and who are more and more on the move. A religious consciousness suitable to the new urban "desert" sect does not offer the securities represented by such conventional religious words as "rock," "bulwark," "bastion" and "fortress," but encourages flexibility. As the ancient Qumran *Manual* says, "This is the time of clearing the way to go to the wilderness."
>
> As a model for the kind of courageous freedom this religious outlook calls for, our studies in Christian origins are more and more bringing to the foreground a flesh-and-blood Jesus (in contrast to the somewhat precious figures

> of the pastel Sunday school pictures and to the dehydrated dogmatic abstractions of the churchly definitions). One emerges who risked daily danger as a leader in the freedom movement of his people. To Israel's source of identity, the Torah, he asserted great loyalty, yet he spontaneously leapt over the wall of the law in order to respond to the hurts or hopes of a person. He was indeed a man for others: for his people *and* for individuals. He is strikingly relevant as a model for the kind of man struggling to come of age in this time of crisis.
>
> Our studies, too, have led us to the conclusion that the most plausible explanation for Jesus' continued influence after his death is the *reality pointed to* by the varied psychic phenomena *experienced* by those close to him, demonstration his ability to continue to transcend space and time. Jesus is the only one of various Messianic figures of that period whose influence grew *after* defeat and death.
>
> We are convinced that Jesus' resurrection plus the experience of expanded awareness, enlightenment or 'cosmic consciousness' that turned a Saul into a Paul are the very foundations upon which Christianity was built. It is this kind of experience of reality that gave the Christian movement its start: the Establishment suppressed it or processed it into arid dogma, and over and over again, its expression has had to break out in less than respectable "heretical sects."

Jesus' Way of Life is an Exodus, in a world oppressed by the sin of people who tend to lord it over one another, to oppress one another, whose guilt we admit in ourselves, whose crying need for liberation we share, whose plight has moved the heart of a merciful God who emptied Himself of all lordship and triumph and came among us in Jesus as one of us, the Suffering Servant of all, promising a life where all people are sisters and brothers: and dying for us that He might rise again among us and in us as the Spirit of Jesus, leaving with us and in us a power, completely beyond the limited powers of our mind, heart and feelings, to help make a creative and free future possible. Thus we can truly and joyouly affirm that we are called together in a common commitment to Jesus our Brother as Messiah and Liberator. He is risen indeed!

Celebrate Life: Yes –
And history yields One Name
in the age-long human Exodus,
One Person by whom we measure
our lives and our celebration:
The Carpenter-Teacher of Nazareth,
Revolutionary of Love
travelling the land
with his band of Disciple-Lovers.
His hand purified the Temple
cleansing Mammon from our lives,
and His love lit eternal flames
to burn all empires down.
Maranatha – Come, Jesus Messiah!
Make your Presence among us.
Peace, always.

We seek in Holy Scripture and in the teaching of our forerunners in this prophetic faith throughout the ages, a Witness to the Word of Truth: to bear witness to the journey from darkness to Light in the revolutionary covenant of Love and freedom brought to us by Jesus and sealed in His blood spilled into the earth against the forces of hatred, violence, oppression, inequality and "the rulers of darkness in the high places of the world." (Eph. 6:12)

St. John tells us that God is love. His very act of being,

His emptying Himself of all triumph, lordship and power to be among us in Jesus and, after the Deed of Golgotha, to remain with us as the Spirit of Jesus, is the supreme act of love. Since the Bible tells us that we are made "in the image and likeness of God," each act of love on our part is a sharing of the divine love and is, itself, something beautiful, sacred, divine.

While we must seek spiritual unity and solidarity among all the Disciples of Jesus, basing such efforts on the great unities of the Faith (listed in Ephesians 4: 3–6): One Body, the Church of Jesus; One Spirit, the creative and holy Spirit of Jesus; One Hope, that of the spiritual fulfillment of history in the creative community of Love through Jesus; One Leader, Jesus our Brother, Messiah and Liberator; One Faith, the following in the way of Jesus; One Baptism, the baptism of the Spirit of Jesus, an initial spiritual experience which joins a person to Jesus and which is made public for us by believers' baptism in water; and One Creator of all, the One who is Love, the One made known to us in Jesus: we must simultaneously work for the coming "reign of the people" (Dan. 7:27), being concerned with the building of a new Christian vision that will tap the spiritual roots within us.

"The new revelation," Berdyaev wrote,

> is certainly not to be thought of as a new religion distinct from Christianity, but as the fulfillment and crowning of the Christian revelation, and the achievement of its true oecumenicity. The revelation of the Spirit cannot be just simply waited for: it depends upon the creative activity of man also. It cannot be understood simply as a new revelation of God to man: it is also a revelation of man to God. This means that it will be a divine-human revelation. The separation and opposition of the divine and the human will be overcome in the Spirit, although the distinction between them will be preserved. This is the crowning

point in the mystical dialectic of the divine
and the human.

WAS JESUS GAY?

For Gay people seeking for this radical transfiguration of the Christian mythos, this "new revelation" of which Berdyaev speaks, a basic question must be, Was Jesus Gay? Back in the early days of Black Consciousness in America, in the days of Marcus Garvey, the African Orthodox Church came into being, receiving its first bishops from the Syro-Antiochan Orthodox Church. At its first Synod, an eighty year old Black woman told Archbishop McGuire, with thears in her eyes, "Bishop, you don't know what this church has meant to me. I know no white man would have died for me." When we ask the question, Was Jesus Gay? we are speaking to a like problem for our Gay brothers and sisters, for ourselves.

Christian hope knows of *koinonia* — fellowship, community. This community is self-giving and self-fulfilling because it is rooted in Jesus. He creates *koinonia* through his self-giving. Knowledge and intimacy join in a unitive act of love and care. The Bible knows of no deeper way to speak about the divine relationship with humanity than *yatha*-intercourse and *xaris*-grace (which in the Hebrew means, literally, the cry of a mother camel for her offspring lost in the desert).

Jesus calls us friends. He fashions a new humanity where there is no male or female, where creative love, equity and mutuality govern all human affairs. In this hope we overcome alienation as through acceptance we call one another into being.

Can Gay people partake in this hope and look to Jesus for strength, support, vision and a way to liberation as full human beings in the Community of Love? We can, only if we recognize that Jesus shares our common lot, shares our perspective and is, therefore, a model for Gay Freedom, rather than a tool of our oppression at others' hands.

Negative attitudes about sexuality were formed, during early Christian history, by world-denying body-hating sense-suspecting views held by Docetists who believed that Jesus was a spiritual being with no body; they taught a dogma that bodily or worldly pleasures and pursuits were "contrary to God." Since 325 C.E., when the Emperor Constantine called into being the so-called Ecumenical Council at Nicaea, and achieved unanimity by driving out dissenting interpreters of the faith at the spear-points of the Emperor's soldiers.

The Eastern Orthodox philosopher-historian Nicholas Zernov wrote of the Church after Nicaea, "In the middle of the fourth century the Church suddenly lost its inner harmony and was split into two hostile factions. Christians who had refused to obey Imperial orders now invoked the secular arm to close down rival places of worship and arrest their clergy. The main cause of this transformation was the abrupt fusion of Church and Empire. The life of the Christian community before Nicaea had been based on freedom, membership of the Church involved sacrifice. Nicaea altered these fundamental conditions: the Church became a privileged body." Since then, the institutional church has always suffered from a number of confusions, contradictions and hang-ups over the human nature of Jesus.

Every so-called "heresy" in Christian history has been the result of the more powerful, victorious (and thus "orthodox") party's insistence that the losers were placing too much emphasis on either the humanity or the divinity of Jesus. For the most part, those who stress the divine nature of Jesus have won the historical struggle, but Christians were never really comfortable with this. The trouble is that the teaching of "the whole and perfect human nature of Jesus," that he was made "true man," is essential to Christian teaching and is a part of every creedal statement.

To backtrack just slightly: In regard to the First so-called "Oecumenical Council" at Nicaea, the Eastern Orthodox theologial-historian, Nicholas Zernov, writes:

> At first glance the contrast between the Church before and after Nicaea seems bewildering. During the first three centuries of its existence

> the Christian community had displayed the power of unity and concord and had won the battle against the Empire. In the middle of the fourth century the same Church suddenly lost its inner harmony and was split into tow hostile factions. Christians who had refused to obey Imperial orders now invoked the secular arm to close down rival places of worship and arrest their clergy. The main cause of this transformation wahs the abrupt fusion of Church and Empire. The life of the Christian community before Nicaea had been based on freedom, membership of the Churcxh involved sacrifice. Nicaea altered tghese fundamental conditions: the Church bacame a privileged body.

The Way *of* Jesus is too severe for those who would compromise with the way of exploitation (Luke 14:27). That is the reason there is a religion *about* Jesus (Matt. 15:8). The Way of Jesus and the Prophets is a Way of, by and for the oppressed peoples of the world (Luke 6:20). That is why sexist and racist oppressors hate it (John 14:30) and the reason agents of oppression pay theologians to rip off the Way and come up with a religion about Jesus and the Prophets and the next life (2 Tim. 4:3). The Prophetic Faith has no good word for oppressors and tyrants (Ex. 9:1). It condemns all oppressors (Isa. 3:15) and demands that the people be freed from bondage (ex. 5:1) and have land and houses (Isa. 5:8), food, clothes, health (Matt. 25: 31–46) and freedom (John 8:32) to usher in the reign of the people. (Dan. 7:27).

Today, as in the time of Daniel, the handwriting is on the wall.

> You have praised the gods of silver and gold, of iron and bronze, of wood and stone, which neither see nor hear nor know, and you have not given glory to God, in whose charge is your very breath and in whose hands are all your

> ways. This is why that hand was sent from His Presence and why it wrote this inscription. And these are the words of the writing which was inscribed: *Mene mene tekel upharsin.* Here is the interpretation: *Mene:* God has numbered the days of your reign and brought it to an end; *tekel:* you have been weighed in the balance and found wanting; *upharsin:* and your nation has been divided and given away from you." (Dan. 5:23–8).

Babylon must fall!

The prophets and Jesus taught that government ought not be allowed to remain in the hands of tyrants (Isa. 9:6). They worked to turn the world system right side up (Luke 1:52), to correct the extremes of sexual division and racial antagonism (Gal. 3:28), of wealth and poverty, by making the first last, and the last first (Matt. 19:30).

Honest readings of the Bible will reveal that throughout history "God has been with the people" (Isa. 62:10), leading the struggle against tyranny and for righteousness, freedom and justice (Isa. 65: 21–5). In the fullness of time there were raised up many leaders (Ex. 2: 10–11) among the oppressed multitudes (Ex. 3:6–10). The history of the Jewish people made it possible for Jesus to become Leader, Messiah and Liberator for all people (Matt. 9:36–8) and to start a movement for a just social order (Luke 14–15). His Community of Love and Liberation, a creative and co-operative commonwealth for all that labor and are heavy-laden and need rest (Matt. 11:28).

The Jews of His time, like Gay people today, were a toiling and persecuted people. Mary, Joseph, Elizabeth, Zacharias, Anna, Simeon, the shepherds and others had become aware of the demonic forces of oppression and alienation that were crushing the people. When Mary knew that she was to become the mother of Jesus, she declared, to use the language of today, her solidarity with those of low status and rejoiced that she was to have a part in the divine liberation of the people of the world. Jesus at the age of twelve confounded the theologians who had forgotten to apply their religion towards the liberation of the people. After this, he worked with Joseph at the carpenter's bench until he was about thirty (Luke: chapters 1–3). He learned the problems of the people at first hand, becoming the servant of all.

Born at a time when a decree was sent out from Caesar that the whole world should be taxed (Luke 2:1), Jesus found the rulers, the politicians and the preachers collaborating (Matt. 22:16) to keep the people subjected to the rule of Rome (Luke 20:20). The historical age of Jesus, the early Roman empire, witnessed violence against personal integrity and against social classes comparable to today's violence. In the absence of technology and without a population explosion strangling the world, the age of Jesus did not see a comparable violence against the ecology. But the symbolism of the end of the physical world which Jesus used as a basis for the ethic of His radical Way shows His prophetic insight that comparable violence against nature was both possible and likely. To defeat this, He knew that all oppressed people must be united (Matt. 5:5) into a world community (Matt. 13:38), and that without regard to sex, race, tribe or tongue (Luke 13:29).

The Son of Humanity was the open spokesperson for an international underground. He spoke in a symbolic language about the insurrection of the just, when the poor would rise from the tomb of slavery in world-wide non-violent revolution, throw off the yoke of Rome and establish the reign of the people. In the Bible, just, poor and righteous are synonymous terms, as also are rich, wicked and unrighteous.

As Bishop (at that time Canon) Hugh Montefiore of the Church of England said,

> It is precisely my concern to show Christ's complete identification with mankind that raises for me a question about our Lord's celibacy. I raise it with reference to those 'thirty hidden years' at Nazareth when it seems that as yet he did not know either his vocation as Messiah or status as

> son of God. Why did he not marry? After all he was fully a man. Of course there is no evidence, and we can only speculate, and speculation must be done with reverence. But having raised the question we must look it in the face — why did he not marry? Could the answer be that Christ was not the marrying sort?... I would wish to claim that this kind of speculation about the nature of our Lord can be valuable if it underlines, as I believe it does here in a particular vivid way, how God in Christ identifies himself with the outsider, and the outcast from society.

Three of the greatest love stories in the Bible concern David and Jonathan, Ruth and Naomi, and Jesus and John. David, one of the ancestors of Jesus, had a love for Jonathan that is related in II Samuel (1:26) as being "greater than (his) love for a woman," and Ruth and Naomi's love is recounted in the Book of Ruth.

Regarding Jesus Himself, the Gospel of John states repeatedly and quite pointedly that John was the disciple "whom Jesus loved" and who laid with his head resting on Jesus' breast at the Last Supper. This Gospel also reports that, while dying on the Cross of Calvary, Jesus committed His widowed mother to His beloved disciple for safety.

Let us also look into the incident of the Centurion's servant as it is related in two of the Gospels (Matt. 8: 5–13; Luke 7: 2–10). This records one of the healings Jesus performed. When he describes Jesus' healing of the Centurion's servant, St. Matthew uses the Greek word "pais" — literally meaning a youth but used often in the writings of the time in specific relation to the youthful lover of an officer in the Roman armies. The Centurion, knowing the disdain of the Jewish authorities of that time for Gay people, said that he was not worthy for Jesus to enter under his roof, and with Jesus' proscriptions against taking part in violence, we may even be somewhat surprised at His healing in this instance. Still, Jesus who, although condemning the sin or violence never condemned the sinner, said in regard to this Centurion that he had not found so great a faith in all of Israel. Never once did Jesus condemn the Centurion; and, for that matter, never once did He make any statement against and homosexual practice.

Likewise, in regard to sexuality in general: in the story of Jesus and the adultress (John 8: 1–11) Jesus Himself offers some guidelines — both by what He says and by what He does not say.

The Pharisees and the Scribes, as they had before, had once again laid a trap for Jesus. According to Jewish law, the woman caught in adultery was supposed to be put to death by stoning (Deut. 22). However, in the Roman province of Palestine, only the Roman governor could pronounce sentence of death — and under Roman law the woman would not have been sentenced to death. Thus, whatever Jesus might say in this instance, He would be "in the wrong." If He said that the woman should be stoned, He would in effect by inciting a lynching. If He said that the woman should not be stoned, He would be showing disrespect for Moses.

Jesus took His time. he kept them waiting while drawing in the sand. Finally He said, "Let him who is without sin cast the first stone." He implied that the self-righteousness of the men who would have stoned this woman was a far greater sin than the one she had committed. This, too, is the thrust of Jesus' baffling words about plucking out the lusting eye and cutting off the straying hand: it is a clear metaphor warning against self-righteousness.

In both of these cases, the Centurion and the Woman caught in adultery, Jesus teaches us to place persons first, at all times. Whatever the Law might say, Jesus reminds us that every situation should be considered specifically, situationally, with respect to an individual human person. Where the Scribes and Pharisees could only see a case for which the Law had a chapter and verse, Jesus saw a person — in one case, the Gay Centurion, in the other, an adultrous woman — a person who was a participant in the life divine. So He said, in the case of the woman, now standing alone before Him: "Neither do I condemn you."

On this subject of the Pharisees, Bishop James Pike remarked that most Christians identify "Pharisees" with "hypocrites" and regard them as generally evil. "This," he said,

> is due to faulty religious education. The truth is that Jesus took the Pharisees seriously and felt it was particularly important to express judgement against them *precisely because* they were the most serious and devout Jews of His day. Some Protestant writers recognize this when they say the Pharisees represent the *status quo* of society. More pointedly, they represent *ourselves* at our most respectable. But we conceive of most stories as having a hero and a villain, and we like to identify ourselves with the hero. Therefore, students of the Bible tend to identify themselves with Christ against the Pharisees. Actually, they should be identifying themselves with the Pharisees, against whom stood — and stands — the judgement of Christ.

In regard to Jesus, we also know that He was unmarried and that all of his closest companions were male. He never condemned nor even spoke directly about Gay people, about homosexuality. He said all the commandments were summed up in two — and both were commandments to Love.

Again, in the Gospel of John, with no hint of jealousy but in explicit terms, John also reports that Jesus loved Lazarus. He cried before the tomb of Lazarus to such an extent that those around Him took it as proof of a very personal love.

He showed some favor to certain women, such as Martha and Mary (the sisters of Lazarus) and Mary of Magdala (who was condemned by others as a harlot); but no relationship with a woman was ever established in the Biblical account that approaches that of Jesus with John.

In the Gospel according to Mark, we are told that Jesus, upon beholding the rich young man, "loved him." Jesus also asked this young man to give up all his wealth and follow Him — but he loved his possessions more than he loved Jesus.

In the Gospel according to Thomas, recently uncovered in Egypt but long known among the Syro-Chaldean Christians in Persia and India, Jesus says: "If you will have cast off the mantle of shame, when you shall be naked without having shame — when you will be two in one body, male and female — then you will know the nature God gave you."

The anti-sexual teaching of Constantinian Christianity finds no grounding in the Way of Life or Words of Jesus. When it does appear in the New Testament, it is in the words of Paul. However, Paul himself insists that he is not the Liberator and that, therefore, his advice does not have any divine, permanent status. Again and again he says, "Remember, this is not Jesus talking but Paul."

Thus Paul is not laying down laws on sexuality. We do not have to accept his opinion that marriage is designed chiefly to keep us from lapsing into immorality nor his statements on homosexuality! There has always been a group of Christians who base their Christianity not on the writings of Paul, but on the Teachings of Jesus. Jesus never condemns anyone — except the hypocrites, those who make an extreme pretense of being very religious. Jesus never condemned those whom the society of His day so freely condemned.

The motivation Jesus sought to instill in people was not that of fear and condemnation, but that of faith and active works of love. In fact, when Jesus spoke of sin, it was the sin of not feeding the poor, not housing the homeless, not taking care of strangers and neglecting the other corporal works of mercy (Matt. 25: 31–46). Beyond that, He said very little about sin but very much about humanity being created in the divine image.

Throughout its history the institutional church has insisted that Jesus did not exercise the power of sex that was rightfully His. Some taught that sex was tainted, the result of original sin: it was beneath the dignity of the sinless Christ. Some taught that since there was no need for children, there was no need for sex. Still others taught that Jesus voluntarily sublimated His sexuality for a greater apostolate. Whatever the reason, safeguarding the divinity of Jesus was basic, and all suggested that sex was not in keeping with holiness.

However, as the Rev. Laud Humphreys said,

> In the light of modern social science, it may be concluded that Jesus must have enjoyed some interpersonal, sexual relationships, complete with orgasm, if he can be said to have shared *fully* in human nature. If, as the Church claims, he is the prime example of the healthy, whole, human personality, he cannot have fought off erections all his life! The Gospels, I think, provide fair indication with whom...he engaged in sexual activity.
>
> Jesus was a pretty radical sort of teacher, concentrating on issues of social justice, combined with a liberal education in theology and the healing arts...Like Socrates before him, Jesus was executed for teaching sedition and heresy, along with corrupting the young.

This brings up Walt Whitman's lines on the subject:

See the philosophies all —
Christian churches and tenets see,
Yet underneath Socrates clearly see —
and underneath Christ the divine I see
the dear love of man for his comrade —
the attachment of friend to friend.

Here is Edward Carpenter, writing in the early decades of the Twentieth Century (and using the terms then current, in which "Uranian" or "child of Uranus" meant what we now mean by "Gay"):

O Child of Uranus, wanderer down all times,
Darkling, from farthest ages of the Earth the same
Strange tender figure, full of grace and pity,
Yet outcast and misunderstood of man —
Thy Woman-soul within a Man's form dwelling,
(Was Adam perchance like this, ere Eve from his side was
drawn?)
So gentle, gracious, dignified, complete,
With man's strength to perform, and pride to suffer
without sign,
And feminine sensitiveness to the last fibre of being;
Strange twice-born, having entrance to both worlds —
Loved, loving by either sex,
And free of all their lore!

I see thee where down all of Time thou comest;
And women break their alabaster caskets, kiss and anoint
thy feet, and bless the womb that bore thee,
While in thy bosom with thee, lip to lip,
Thy younger comrade lies.

Lord of the love which rules this changing world,
Passing all partial loves, this one complete —
the Mother-love and sex-emotion blended —
I see thee where for centuries thou hast walked,
Lonely, the world of man,
Saving, redeeming, drawing all to thee,
Yet outcast, slandered, pointed of the mob,
Misjudged and crucified.
Dear Son of heaven — long-suffering wanderer through
the wilderness of civilization —
The day draws nigh when from these mists of ages
Thy form in glory clad shall reappear.

Yes, Jesus could have been Gay on the basis of historical data, but the evidence, in terms of overt homosexual behavior, will never be conclusive. What is crystal clear, however, is that Jesus was one who came to save the oppressed, to relate to those whom society has cast out and to be a model for their liberation. He did not, ever, say "Get on your knees and worship me;" He said "Follow me." He said He came "to bring life more abundant," (John 10:10), "to bring the Good News to the poor; to proclaim liberty to the captives; to the unseeing, new vision; to those in bondage, freedom; to the oppressed, liberation; to all, the time of the Liberator's favor." (Luke 4:18). Above all, He held up *agape,* self-giving love, as the commandment to both challenge and perfect all commandments.

Although Jesus, by His Presence with the revolutionaries of His day, recognized the justice of their cause, every bit of His teaching and life-style consistently proclaim that the liberated society will be created, finally, only through reconciling, creative and nonviolent Love. And in His first message at Nazareth (Luke 4:18) He declared His Oneness with the people and announced that His purpose on earth was to carry out an uncompromising struggle against all tyrants and their practices (John 10:10).

To be effective in this struggle, Jesus recognized the need for a broader approach than official Israel had taken (Matt. 23:13); and He openly stated that He would include in this revolutionary community people from among all groups, as Elias and Eliseus had done in the time of famine and plague (Luke 4: 25–7). He took His cause directly to Gays (the Centurion), Women (the Samaritan women, Mary of Magdala, Mary and Martha), workers (Luke 4:30–32) and other victims of the world-empire (Matt. 21:31). He was of the people, knew their problems and spoke their language (John 10: 14-16). The oppressed heard Him gladly (Mark 12:37). They thronged about Him as He entered Jerusalem (Matt. 21: 9–15) where he boldly condemned all who oppress the people (Matt. chapter 23) or who compromise with oppressive practices (Luke 22: 25–6).

He taught us the Way of Liberation of the Good News as He gave us His new commandment: to love one another as He loved us. His announcement of this creative principle of revolutionary, nonviolent Love marks Him out as fulfilling the highest expectation of all religion, as providing the pattern most urgently called for by our own times and as illustrating the true and ultimate character of humanity (Eph. 4:13).

But His revelation of reconciling nonviolence and radical Love brought Him into conflict with both those who sought compromise with Imperial Rome for their own comfort and with those whose revolution merely sought for the violent overturn of Imperial power and its replacement with their own power.

Seeing that Jesus was gaining a following (John 12:19), the politicians planned to mob Him (Matt. 26: 3–5). They were afraid to arrest Him on fake charges lest there be an uprising (Mark 14: 1–2). They therefore covenanted with a double-minded disciple to deliver Him into their hands (Luke 22: 3–6). Seized at night while the people slept, given a mock trial (Matt. 26: 59–66) before daybreak, they demanded His death. He was killed on the Cross of a political prisoner (Luke 23: 44) as the Leader of the peoples' movement for liberation (Luke 23:5) — crucified under Pontius Pilate, Caesar's political henchman (Luke 23: 24) at the request of influential religious leaders (Mark 15:1).

Jesus was executed as a political conspirator, a revolutionary: but by the Deed of His Blood spilled into the earth, the world is held together and restored to its sanctity, and the foundations are laid for our liberation from the bondage of sin — violence, exploitation and oppression — and our growth into that liberated Paradisal community in which we were meant to live our lives creatively. The forces of oppression had killed Jesus, but He had established a movement for economic, sexual, racial, religious and political justice against which all the tyrannies of hell could not prevail (Matt. 16:18). What *was* most passionate, real and lasting about Jesus *is* precisely His radical humanity.

By the Deed of Golgotha Jesus has imbedded Himself deep in the fabric of the profane world; and by His resurrection He broke with finality the bonds of darkness that He might lead us into His perfect Light: raising us to that sharing in the Divine Life which is the life of the Liberated Community of Love. He is truly in the world, in the neighbor, in the whole creation. He is the heart of the struggle against war and division, against violence and confusion, against sexism, racism and imperialism, and for peace, clarity and unification. The Victim of sin became the Victor and won the victory over sin, death, oppression and disunity of all people. He is in humanity and we are all members of His Body. In one sense, it is true as Oscar Wilde says in *De Profundis*, that "Christ does not really teach one anything, but by being brought into His Presence one *becomes* something. And everybody is predestined to His Presence. Once at least in his life every man walks with Christ to Emmaus."

The radical Jesus claims to beckon us as Gay people today. And as it is a *call to our liberation* not on straight men's terms, but on Gay people's terms, it is indeed a Gay Jesus who is doing this beckoning.

THE CHURCH OF THE FIRST-BORN: TOWARDS A RADICAL GAY CHRISTIAN COMMUNITY

The Church, the Community of Jesus, is those people in the world who are committed to breaking the bonds of their own oppression in a manner that affirms their basic humanity and right to franchise over their own existence. Pierre Teilhard de Chardin, the Jesuit priest and scientist, writes that the person who is "filled with an impassioned love of Jesus hidden in the forces which bring increase to the Earth, him the Earth will lift up like a mother in the immensity of her arms, and will enable him to contemplate the face of God."

The Spirit of Jesus calls us to a revolution of transforming Love: a Way of Life to which the Good News bears witness as it assures us of Jesus' promises by the gifts of His Spirit to His Community. Only by accepting those gifts which have been promised by Jesus to His disciples can we truly transcend our limited selves, experience His Presence and bring into manifestation a society based on the Gospel's revolution and the testimony of the Spirit that in Jesus, all are one. To be one in Jesus means to do His Work in the world.

In his *Meditation on Draft-File Burnings at Catonsville,* the Jesuit priest and war resister Daniel Berrigan wrote:

> We say: killing is disorder. Life and gentleness and community and unselfishness are the only order we recognize. For the sake of that order we risk our liberty, our good name. The time is past when good men may be silent, when obedience can segregate man from public risk, when the poor can die without defence. How many indeed must die before our voices are heard; how many must be tortured, dislocated, starved, maddened? How long must the world's resources be raped in the service of legalized murder? When, at what point, will you say *no* to this [present] war? We have chosen to say with the gift of our liberty, if necessary our lives: the violence stops here, the death stops here, the suppression of the truth stops here, the war stops here. Redeem the times! The times are inexpressibly evil. Christians pay conscious, indeed religious tribute to Caesar and Mars by the approval of overkill tactics, by brinkmanship, by nuclear liturgies, by racism, by support of genocide. They embrace their society with all their heart and abandon the cross. They pay lip service to Christ and military service to the powers of death. And yet, and yet, the times are inexhaustibly good, solaced by the hope and courage of many. The truth rules. Christ is not forsaken. In a time of death some men, the resisters, those who work hardily for social change, those who preach and embrace the truth, such men overcome death, their lives are bathed in the light of the resurrection, the truth has set them free. In the jaws of death, they proclaim their love of their brethren. We think of such men in the

> world, in our nation, in the churches, and the stone in our breast is dissolved: we take heart once more.

In our day, the church bearing Jesus' Name has few prophetic voices to sound above the noises of violence and destruction, of sexism and racism. Perhaps, in large part, this is because the church has lost the Spirit which empowered it with strength for struggle against the leviathan forces of the State before Nicaea: not entirely lost, however, for there have always been those who resisted both the violence of the State and the oppressiveness of the institutional Church to stand fast in the Good News of Jesus and to seek to transform the world by His revolutionary Love.

Where the Church's attempts to live again in the Way of Jesus, exploring new paths of application of His revolution in the world, it has often been called an experiment: but wherever the Church is true to its mission it will be experimenting, blazing raw paths, seeking how to apply that revolution and to speak the reconciling Word of Jesus to its own age. As George McLeod, the founder of the Iona Community, writes:

> I simply urge that the Cross be raised again at the center of the marketplace as well as on the steeple of the Church. I am recovering the claim that Jesus was not crucified in a cathedral between two candles, but on a cross between two thieves; at the town garbage heap; at a crossroad so cosmopolitan that they had to write His title in Hebrew and in Latin and in Greek...at the kind of place where cynics talk smut, and thieves curse and soldiers gamble. Because that is where He died. And that is what he died about. And that is where churchmen ought to be and what churchmen ought to be about.

Life and Spirit frighten those in power since they have become the perpetuators of destruction: they would prefer that the cross of Jesus be confined to cathedrals. Whenever the people begin to get it together, Jesus is in their midst, and that Life and Spirit begin to multiply by the thousands.

The social-religious complex fears the organizing of oppressed people: they particularly fear Gayness. That's the reason why unscrupulous machinations against our very being continue to this very day. If compassion were shown to Gay people at any level in church or state, it would cause such an incompatibility with their conceptions of "norm" and "nature" that they would have to re-evaluate their own thinking and perhaps have to change their life-style to walk in the Way of the revolutionary Jesus.

And so, by rejecting us as "immoral," they save face and hide from possible ruination and exposure: a ruination by the standards of Babylon which would be true life by the standards of Jesus; an exposure not only of their lies, but an exposure to the purifying Truth of Jesus. But for these many centuries of oppressing Gays they have had a lingering, unvoiced fear: a fear that says something *might* come along and upset the applecart. It has now come! It's called fury — otherwise known as Gay Freedom. Empowered by the Spirit of Jesus, what a might that is!

Now, if the Church is to keep the Faith, her obstructions must be liberated.We are called to follow in the Way of Jesus, who is not a temple dweller nor imprisoned in cloistered sanctuaries, but He who has broken all bonds and is alive in all persons, at work in all creation. By the pattern of His comings, we are called to seek Him especially among the oppressed, the rejected, the outcast and the poor. We know as His own all those who suffer brokenness of heart, mind, body, dignity and relationships. To all of these, suffering their powerlessness in the world, we dare not go except as brothers and sisters who have nothing to lose, who seek ot gain nothing and who expect to receive far more than we offer, although we offer our all. It must be clear that the transformation we seek comes through Jesus' Presence among us.

Jesus comes to rescue humanity from more than just private and individual misdeeds for which each person is more or less personally responsible. Ultimately, Jesus comes to break the power of that collective and transcendent evil of sexism, racism and people lording it over each other which humanity raises up out of collective exploitiveness and self-enclosure. This kind of collective evil is of the sort that no individual is really responsible for. It is caused by that faceless and omnipresent "they" who are at the same time both everyone and no one in particular. This is the power of the "demonic" which, while originating in collective human will, is a power over which human will has lost control and to which humanity at large has fallen casualty. Even those who are obviously its beneficiaries are as much its slaves and victims as those who are its chief targets.

In the old terms, then, Jesus comes as an exorcist; and one of the basic signs of His Presence is the act of breaking the power of the "demonic" over human life. (In the rituals of the Medieval church, the power of exorcism lay not in any magical power but simply in the act of recognition of the "demon" for what it was. Traditional rituals of exorcism all began with words such as these: "Depart evil spirit...we recognize you for what you are." In that act of recognition, the "demon," who ever lies and dissembles and represents himself as an angel of light, is unmasked and deprived of its power over human life.) True exorcism is the activity of total humanity present in the person, the activity of Love. It is the activity of personhood beyond the ego, where life is without competitiveness and lordship. This is where Jesus is present as we are, that we may be as He is, and we experience wholeness, both of one's own being and of that being's integration with the whole of life. As St. Clement of Alexandria says: "The Word of God became man, so that you might learn from man how man becomes God."

The way forward would seem to be through a new Ecclesia, a revolutionary Church. That is, to become a people called out of established society to accomplish a particular purpose: and that purpose is nothing less than the rebuilding of society from the bottom upwards — a total rejection of the obscenity of sexism, racism, violence, acquisitiveness and competition. As people get sickened by the way we live now, so there will emerge small groups who will want to heal their alienation with real love and community. It is our task to help such groups to get started — to help provide the basis for them and to nurture them when they are getting started.

The liberation of Gay people, the liberation of all people, may well be dependent upon such a meditation on the symbols of the Christian faith as that called for by Carl Jung and the World Council of Churches, and upon a transformation of the spiritual values of our world through a truly religious struggle for a world-wide co-operative commonwealth, a creative society in which body and spirit are reunited. That struggle cannot be carried out alone, but must be entered into by Gay brothers and sisters as a Radical Gay Christian Community, a Revolutionary Church seeking to be faithful to the heritage of Jesus as received from His disciples through the ages, and asserting as our special vocation the primary task of serving the Gay Community from within — not as missionaries, but as Radical Gay Christians coming together to create love, support and identity among all Gay brothers and sisters. We are called, as Berdyaev says:

> to act as though you could hear the Divine Call to participate through free and creative activity in the Divine Work; to... struggle with evil in yourself and around you – not in order to relegate the wicked to hell and create a kingdom of evil, but to conquer evil and to further a creative regeneration of the wicked.... Every moral act of love... brings to pass the end of the world where hatred, cruelty and selfishness reign supreme. Every creative act entails the promise of a new, an "other" world, where power is revealed in freedom and in love.

Such a Radical Gay Christian Church must seek to apply the insights of the apostolic and primitive Church Community of Jesus to the needs of contemporary Gay people: offering the Bread of Life to those who never before have been offered anything but the stones of rejection, neglect and oppression. In the turmoil of this oppression, in the face of this rejection and neglect, in the center of the cyclone that is our struggle for freedom, we hear the Call of the Bible: "You are a people holy to the Lord your God, and the Lord has chosen you out of all peoples on earth to be His special people" (Deut. 14:2). "We are no more strangers and foreigners, but fellow-citizens with the saints and of the household of God; and are built upon the foundation of the apostles and prophets, Jesus Christ Himself being the chief cornerstone" (Eph. 2:19-20). This is not to say that Gay people alone are the chosen people of the Old and New Covenants, but that Gay people, and all people seeking liberation, are called to "prepare a people that shall be fit for the Liberator" (Luke: 1:17). "God's own words are: 'I will live and move about among them; I will be their God and they shall be my people.' And therefore, 'come out from among them and be a separate people,' says the Lord" (2 Cor. 6:16–17). As Rosemary Ruether says: "to join the church is to separate out from the world and to stand as the avant-garde of a new world that is being founded by God in the midst of the old world that is dying."

It must be understood that the word *Gay* as used here, while starting from a base of accepting homosexuality, does not exclusively refer to sexual gender preference, but rather defines a life-style in which love, trust and support among all people supplant relationships based on hate, fear and competitive aggression. Gay is a process of attaining mutual and equal social and sensual relationships among all human beings. This universality of Gay Love and of the struggle for liberation was foreshadowed by the Prophet Daniel when he wrote of the coming "reign of the people" (Dan. 7:27); by John the Beloved Disciple of Jesus when he wrote "... by your blood you did purchase for God persons of every tribe and language, people and nation: you have made of them a royal house, to serve our God as priests, and they shall reign upon earth." (Rev. 5:9); and by Abbot Joachim of Fiore, writing at the end of the Thirteenth Century: "Life should be changed because the state of the world will be changed. We shall not be what we have been, but we shall begin to be other."

Without too much trouble, you can walk through the streets of any city in America at almost any hour, day or night, and see the desolate, alienated and oppressed people. Take a moment to talk to adolescent runaways, homeless youth, street people, Black people, Latin Americans and Indian Americans, the aged, the handicapped, draft resisters, demonstrators for peace and revolutionaries who feel that the institutional church has betrayed the message of the Gospel; speak with Gay people — homosexuals, bisexuals and people seeking to know Love in any of its many diverse forms — who have been rejected by the institutional church that has refused to admit that Love, any kind of Love, is the reflection of the Love shown in Jesus, and learn the alienation of an entire cross-section of our population.

No longer are paternalistic and bureaucratic missions able to buy off angry and alienated people with platitudes and "Sunday-go-to-meeting" religion. It is precisely in this place and at this time that an alternative ministry and mission in the life-style of Jesus as Person for others is most desperately needed for the multitude of alienated people. Our survival may well depend on our ability to overcome past inadequacies and introduce anew Jesus' spiritual revolution.

Such a ministry must address the causes of alienation: interpersonal violence, sexism, racism, war; emotional repression; impersonal bureaucracy, injustice and corruption in high office; manipulation of personal freedom. The alternative is a Community of serving the people, following in the sometimes bloody footsteps of Jesus as the Person for others and sharing in the lives and life-style of those being served.

While more often than not the institutional church sells out its Pearl of Great Price to property, status, social position, money and the military-industrial-academic establishment, an alternative Community can serve as the steward of that Pearl.

While the institutional church often silences its witness rather than lose its position and wealth, an alternative Community has the possibility of witness precisely because it has no wealth and no position. While the institutional church trades in the offensive Jesus for a new, comfortable, machine-made model, an alternative Community has the possibility of being His Body in the world; a friend of the outsider and the underdog, enemy of hypocrisy and violence.

While the institutional church makes of the scandal of the Gospel a comfortable pew, an alternative Community has in it the possibility of proclaiming the Gospel which is an outrageous shout of Love and Joy!

While the institutional church condemns Gay revolution, an alternative Community has the possibility of recognizing therein the Speech of Jesus.

While the institutional church takes itself so seriously that it hardens and dies, an alternative Community has the possibility of learning how to play and celebrate, and therefore how to truly worship.

While the institutional church is safe, an alternative Community risks persecution, martyrdom, prison, sainthood and victory in the transformation of the world into a loving and creative Community of all humanity in the Spirit of Jesus.

In this alternative Community, fellowship is filled with the rush of a mighty wind, a tongue of fire over every head. Then we can go out from this Community with the power of the Spirit of Jesus, and change the world. If we don't put this Community together, nobody else will, and our sisters and brothers will be destroyed. And if they are destroyed, we will be destroyed with them, perhaps by them.

And so it is: for the Gospel, the Good News of Jesus our Brother, calls to "the least of these, my brothers and sisters" (Matt. 25). As part of the world movement, we are called to come together as a free-standing and liberating Radical Gay Christian Community in which all people find themselves accepted as they are. The Church's task is not to save itself —

Jesus has already done that. It is rather to give itself in love and service — in fact, to die for the world.

The Way of Life in Jesus has two functions: external and internal. The external function is the outward reach in love and service, in relationship, in the sharing and expression of Jesus' Love in action, towards all humanity and all of the cosmos. It is a commitment in the Name of Jesus "to bring Good News to the poor, to proclaim liberty to the captives, to proclaim new vision to the unseeing, to proclaim freedom to those in bondage, to proclaim liberation to the oppressed, to proclaim to all the time of the Liberator's favor." In its internal function this takes the form of work on oneself, the search within one's own depths for union with Jesus, with the Life Divine. Our worship is in our service. Through our following the example of self-sacrifice in the service of others, our lives become assimilated to Jesus' Life in ways which we cannot understand but which we experience as His Spirit breaks through into our consciousness.

The Sacraments of Jesus' liberating Community of Love serve as the bridge between these external and internal functions, giving us strength for struggle both in ourselves and in the world. In the words of St. Dionysius the Areopagite:

> Now the first effect of the sacraments, manifesting the action of God in its symbolic form, is to purify the imperfect; the second is to illuminate and initiate those whom it has purified; its last, which includes and fulfils the two preceding, to perfect the initiate in the knowledge of the Mysteries to which they have access.

Sacraments are the self-impartation of the Love of Jesus in the form of action.

Friedrich Heiler, late Syro-Chaldean Bishop in Germany, wrote:

> In His brief and scattered remarks about true and false prayer, Jesus has described His very self. His sharp criticism of the prayer-methods of the hypocrites and the heathen gives us an outlook on the fashion of His own praying. The hypocrites pray at the corners of the streets; He prays in His inner chamber... on His knees throughout the livelong night. His injunction to pray for our enemies springs out of His own prayer-life; even on the Cross He intercedes for His murderers.

A true prayer life and inner work must bear fruit in works to others: but works of service and action for social change, unless they proceed from inner transformation, are of real and lasting benefit to none. Each of us must undertake the long and difficult — and joyous! — process of living the life: as we have worshipped Jesus in prayer and sacrament, now we must go out and seek Him in every face.

Now we, Gay followers of Jesus, take up this Call and challenge, joining our own liberation struggle with that of women, children, third world peoples, and all the oppressed. We bring the matter, first, before the Community of Faith. We call upon those who call themselves followers of Jesus to bear witness with us to the systematic destruction of our humanity. We call upon those who call themselves the Community of Love to immediately — not cautiously or at some distant day — take measures to undo what has been and to terminate *now* the continuing oppression.

The Church of Jesus has been called "to comfort the afflicted and afflict the comfortable." But the churches of institutional christendom have been more interested in "afflicting the afflicted and comforting the comfortable." We call upon the Community of Faith and Love to remember Jesus, the subject or "Thou" of its Faith and its first Love, in the oppressed ones of the earth: to renew its commitment and throw itself into the arena to actively and fearlessly serve the people.

We are in a position written of by Jean Cocteau:

> I must be a better Christian than Catholic. I confess I was shocked by the vine leaves on the statues in the Vatican. But I would have thought it normal for the precious stones of the collection to be hidden by vine leaves. I thought of the sentence of Maurras, quoted by Gide, 'I will not leave the learned procession of reverend fathers, councils, popes and all the great men of modern times, in order to concentrate on the Gospels of four obscure Jews.' This is an extreme expression of anti-Semitism...What can I say? This is the way I am built. I hate only hatred.

Unlike Charles Maurras, but like Cocteau in this call he issued, we shall leave "the procession of councils and popes, in order to concentrate on the Gospels of four obscure Jews." Jesus our Brother, Messiah and Liberator, Himself just such an "obscure Jew," calls us to be true to the Good News and to his nonviolent revolution of reconciling Love: to be true to the transforming and creative work of His Spirit operating inwardly in every person as the Indwelling Light, operating in the Community of His Way as the Sacramental Life, and operating in the world as the Revolutionary Movement for Peace, Freedom, Social Justice and Human Dignity for *all* people. We are called to stand in ecumenical solidarity with all others engaged in that struggle and movement, whether religious or secular, whatever they call themselves, and to recognize their Work as the true service and ministry of the people that is the heart of the Gospel of Jesus and the Prophets. We are called to proclaim Jesus our Brother as the Center of the universe and our Symbol of Human-ness, Hope, Love and Justice: and to proclaim the New Age, the Realm of the Rising Bread (as it was called both in Scripture and during the French Revolution), the Reign of the People, the Commonwealth of Peace and Justice that is the Permanent Gospel promised by Jesus. Bearing witness in our sacramental life — to the Celebration of Life in Jesus our Brother as Presence for us — we are called to seek in dialogue with other Liberation movements and other revolutionary movements in religion around the world for the way to a liberated humanity in a liberated world. For us, this is a world of peace and human love anticipated at the Table of Jesus our Brother!

We must create and nurture such a Community, as a symbol to others that people can come together. Otherwise our words, our commitments, our dreams remain unsubstantiated.

We must live what we believe because, in Berdyaev's words, "The question of bread for myself is a material question; The question of bread for my neighbor is a spiritual and religous question."

Every compromise that we make raises doubts as to not only the practical possibilities of our beliefs (those doubts would be tolerable, for we are called upon to be "fools for Christ") but also how important our beliefs are to us. Talking a better way but compromising with oppression is what churches, governments and reformers have done throughout history. All the talk — backed by so little reality — has made doubt, fear and disillusionment the hallmarks of our age.

What really matters to us — what we really believe — is shown by the way we live. We cannot talk our way to a consecrated and fulfilled humanity. Only the obvious reality of individuals living rightly will give others the courage to do the same. At the time of Jesus, Rabbi Hillel said, "If I am not for myself, who will be? If I am only for myself, what am I? And if not now, when?" And the Bible answers, "Now is the time of choice, now is the day of liberation!" (2 Cor. 6:2)

You can change the world: we are all a part of life. As Daniel Berrigan says:

> Who would be my teacher? It was, finally, the world. It was the world we breathe in, the only

> stage of redemption, the men and women who toil in it, sin in it, suffer and die in it. Apart from them, as I came to know, the priesthood was a pallid, vacumatic enclosure, a sheepfold for sheep.

Radical Gay Christians are called by the Spirit of Jesus to provide an ecumenical and sacramental community of reconciliation for social involvement, both in the revolutionary movement for transformation and in the collective fulfilment of human needs, from finding shelter for those on the streets and food for those who are hungry, to providing peer-counselling and comfort to those in spiritual or psychological need. We are called to administer the Word and the Sacraments of Jesus' Community of Love, and to provide means for human encounter and growth. All of humanity's past failures are not enough to destroy our hope and belief that we can create a better world wherein it will be a constant joy to draw the breath of life. In the words of the Submarine Church Press (Nov. 1970):

> Through our collective struggle we Gay folk of the land will emerge with a new self-awareness and pride in ourselves, in what we stand for, and in the battle which all oppressed people are now fighting. The future revolutionary society, towards which a Radical Gay Christian Church or Community must aim, is a society whose future details we can not label or blueprint. We should, by now, have learned from the example of the revolutionaries of the past that when you begin the labeling process for the future society, you end the awareness of the continuity of consciousness, the continuity of the dialectic, and you cut yourself off from contact with the Spirit and struggle in the here-and-now. Freedom is not an end, freedom is a process.

At the beginning of the twentieth century, Edward Carpenter, resigned Anglican priest, libertarian socialist, mystic, prophet of the Gay Freedom Movement, wrote:

> It is possible that the Uranian (i.e. Gay) spirit may lead to something like a general enthusiasm of Humanity, and that the Uranian people may be destined to form the advance guard of that great movement which will one day transform life by substituting the bond of personal affection and compassion for the monetary, legal and other external ties which now confine and control society. Such a part of course we cannot expect the Uranians to play unless the capacity for their kind of attachment also exists — though in a germinal and undeveloped state — in the breast of humanity at large. And modern thought and investigation are clearly tending that way — to confirm that it does so exist.

The Episcopal priest Robert O. Weeks writes:

> The Gay Power Movement in this country is the latest in a series of protests against centuries of wrong treatment and social injustice: we have seen the Black and the Chicano and the American Indian and, finally, the American Woman. Now we have to see the Homosexual as a person whom we have treated unfairly from the beginning. Gay Power advocates might congratulate themselves that they are, in fact, making important history, and facing the nation with its unfinished homework.

Freedom is not an end: freedom is a process. What we've got to do, in following the Radical Jesus, is to engage in the struggle fully, here and now. To quote from Vancouver Gay Liberation:

> We should not seek to fit into this culture, this dying nation of *Playboy* pinups and stinking rivers. We do not want to prove that we can make better marriages, cops or businessmen than straights. We owe this culture nothing but our determination to replace it.

We need joy to move ahead. Let us search it out. Let us, above all, experience it.

— Los Angeles, June 1972

– II –
LIBERATION IN LOVE

A Meditation on the Prayer of Jesus
Commonly called The Lord's Prayer

Our Father who art in heaven
Hallowed by thy name.
Thy kingdom come.
Thy will be done,
        on earth as it is in heaven.
Give us this day our daily bread;
And forgive us our sins,
        as we forgive every one
        who is indebted to us;
And lead us not into temptation,
But deliver us from evil.
(Matthew 6: 8–13; Luke 11: 2–4)

John Parman Brown, Episcopal priest and theologian of the Berkeley Free Church and the San Francisco Ecumenical Peace Institute writes:

> Matthew's first three clauses all mean the same. The coming of the Kingdom *is* the fulfilment of the will of God for justice in history; it also conforms and validates his true character or "name." (The name of a person in ancient lan-

guages is a whole phrase thought of as defining their true self.)

"Daily" perhaps means "for tomorrow": the next day began at sunset, after which the one full meal was taken. Then the meaning is: during the day we worry about the bread for that evening only. — Luke's *sins* is a correct interpretaton of the Aramaic idiom in "debts."

"Temptation" may be better translated "time of testing."

The Aramaic original was probably in meter. One possible reconstruction could be rendered:

FATHER:
BLESSED BE YOUR WORKING;
SOON BE YOUR APPEARING;
DONE BY YOUR DESIRING.
OUR BREAD PROVIDE US;
OUR DEBTS FORGIVE US;
FROM TRIALS FREE US.

With that introduction from Dr. Brown, we shall go on to our

MEDITATION ON THE PRAYER OF JESUS.

OUR FATHER,
WHO ART IN HEAVEN,
HALLOWED BE THY NAME.

Our Father, Who is in the highest and the lowest, the first and the last, Your Name is on the heavens and the earth, for You are all. We know Your fatherly love: "He shall cover you with His feathers and under His wings you shall trust: His Truth shall be your shield and armor." We bless and praise Your Name as we follow in Jesus' Way of Life, serving all of humanity.

THY KINGDOM COME.
THY WILL BE DONE
ON EARTH AS IT IS IN HEAVEN.

Your Kingdom — Jesus' Liberated Community of Love — is among us when we work together to bring about Your nonviolent revolution of Love, seeing which, we may enter into Your wholeness and Your perfection: "The Kingdom of God does not come from looking for it; and you shall not say, Here it is! Or, There it is! For behold, the Kingdom of God is among you..... Wherever two or three are gathered in my Name, I am with them." Your Will is the creative Spirit in the heavens and the earth.... Only by serving the people in Your Way of Life can we count ourselves citizens of Your Commonwealth. As Peter and the other apostles said, "We must obey God rather than men."

GIVE US THIS DAY OUR DAILY BREAD.

As we grow in Jesus' Community of Love abundance is made available to us, for we share all things in Him, receiving unfailing supply for every need. You are our inexhaustible supply, feeding us with Living Bread and clothing us with your Way of Life: "And all that believed were together and had all things common... and distribution was made to every person as there was need."

AND FORGIVE US OUR TRESPASSES,
AS WE FORGIVE THOSE WHO TRESPASS AGAINST US.

You have always given us Yourself for ourselves and the strength to transcend our brokenness in receiving Your wholeness. The power of Your New Life is to encounter our brothers and sisters in Jesus and no longer dissemble before them. We know that by numerous acts we have broken the bond of community and sinned by our complicity with the demonic forces of exploitation, divisiveness, destruction, violence and death:

we have shared in the sins of sexism and racism. Yet as we take up Jesus' New Life-Style we are forgiven. Likewise, we must forgive our enemies and work to bring them around to creative nonviolence through Your revolution of Love.... "Love your enemies, bless those who curse you, do good to them that hate you, pray for them who are spiteful to you and persecute you, that you may be the children of your heavenly Father.... Be you perfect, as He is perfect."

LEAD US NOT INTO TEMPTATION, BUT DELIVER US FROM EVIL.

You have always sent before us the task of accepting our wholeness in Jesus, whereby we are delivered from alienation. Yet everywhere the demonic forces of sexism, racism, destructiveness, oppression, alienation and violence surround us and, if we submit, dehumanize us. But You have promised us: "Lo, I am with you always, even to the fulfilment of the ages." By the Spirit of Jesus you make us holy, giving us strength to carry out your nonviolent revolution against the manifold evils of the world. When any person is oppressed, we must speak out and act: if this means jail, then jail is where we find our freedom. If the police are going to brutalize nonviolent protests with clubs and mace, then we must stand in the front line. If young men refuse induction into the military or burn their draft cards, we must stand with them and say "If you are to take them, you take us too." It is in standing with our brothers and sisters in this struggle that You protect us from the temptation to self-satisfaction and complacency, and liberate us from all evil; and we bear within our lives Your call to communicate the Good News of reconciling Love and Peace. "For we do not wrestle against flesh and blood, but against princes, against powers, against the rulers of the darkness of this world, against the spiritual wickedness in high places. So take the whole armor of God... and having done all, stand firmly."

And then we may add the traditional Doxology:

For Thine Is the Kingdom
The Power
And The Glory
Forever.
Amen.

For Yours — ours — is the Kingdom, the Liberated Community of Love; the Power, the strength of wholeness in the emptying of all triumph and lordship; and the Glory of the new and free creation. That Kingdom, Power and Glory faces us with a choice: Christ or the State! We must choose each day which we will serve. "I have set before you life and death, a blessing and a curse! Therefore choose life, that you and your seed shall live." "No man can serve two masters, for he will hate the one and love the other, or else he will hold to the one and despise the other. You cannot serve God and mammon." Jesus our Brother, Messiah and Liberator, is not a lord of withdrawal from the sphere of social action: but He is the Leader of revolution against all vested bureaucracy, the Leader of challenge and nonviolent revolution. Jesus who sweated and bled and understood the stench of sin and who leads us out of darkness into His perfect Light, granting us His creative Spirit to give us wholeness, holiness, in our free and loving life-styles: Jesus our Brother, the revolutionary Carpenter of Nazareth crucified for our liberation and transformation. Maranatha! Come, Jesus Messiah! And so it is.

— New York City
June 1969, after Stonewall
Revised: Los Angeles, May 1972

Editors' notes: This edition of *The Radical Jesus and Gay Consciousness* has been taken (with some editorial revisions) from the second edition, published by Communiversity West in 1972 under the General Editorship of David Barker. The editors would like to thank Rev. Donald Mader for his assistance.

Since 1972 there have been published many popular and scholarly treatments of themes addressed in Bishop Itkin's pioneering work. Here are a few excellent and relatively recent ones:

The Man Jesus Loved: Homoerotic Narratives from the New Testament by Theodore W. Jennings, Jr.; 2003, The Pilgrim Press, 700 Prospect Avenue East, Cleveland, OH 44115–1100; www.pilgrimpress.com.

Reasonable and Holy: Engaging Same-Sexuality by Tobias Stanislas Haller, BSG; 2009, Seabury Books, 445 Fifth Avenue, New York, NY 10016; www.churchpublishing.org.

Radical Love: An Introduction to Queer Theology by Patrick S. Cheng; 2011, Seabury Books (see above); www.patrickcheng.net.

AFTERWORD: COMMUNITY AS LEGACY

ITKIN FOR OUR TIME

Michael Elliot Bacon

> The way forward would seem to be through a new Ecclesia, a revolutionary Church. That is to become a people called out of established society to accomplish a particular purpose: and that purpose is nothing less than the re-building of society from the bottom upwards — a total rejection of the obscenity of sexism, racism, the violent, acquisitive and competitive society. As people get sickened by the way we live now, so will there emerge small groups who will want to heal their alienation with real love and community. It is our task to help such groups to get started — to help provide the basis for them and to nurture them when they are getting started.

Mikhail Itkin states the above in his 1972 *The Radical Jesus and Gay Consciousness: Notes for a Theology of Gay Liberation.* Does this idea of "community" seem credible or laughable in the first decade of the 21st century? If expressed at all, ideas of community are now rare in public discourse. In fact the most informed today may well be those who subscribe to Mrs. Thatcher's widely admired dictum: "There is no such thing as society. There are only individuals and families." Or, so to say, competition is our community; all against one and one against all.

While the space of time from Itkin's writing to the present is short, and the change in operant conditions is great, Itkin's call is as current now as then. The need for community is in fact more acute, even as its conceptualization slips into obscurity.

At the time Itkin wrote the above, his language would have been both new and familiar. To think in wider perspectives was new, but it was "catching-on" quickly. Thousands of such analyses and programs presented people with the challenge that where in society a problem is identified, there also is a solution for it. It was a time when anything felt possible. Because of the war in Vietnam, the civil-rights movement, the emergence of another "left," and especially the gay-rights movement, the patina of society had been scraped away and all inherited values were opened for scrutiny.

His idea, that an Ecclesia or church could be the vehicle of revolution, would itself certainly have received scrutiny. Established religion had on the whole suffered from the "movement." However, it would have been, and was, embraced by many for whom spirituality is necessary for bringing revolutionary change both to society and inwardly. Itkin demonstrated a keen understanding of the times with his projection of a new church. Many experiments in spirituality flourished in the nation. He was also right in saying that small groups would have the best chance of developing a critique, a common life, and sufficient built-in support to make its risky doings feasible.

Receptivity was in the air. Itkin himself would head groups with at times 2,000–3,000 adherents. The question of how successful these ultimately were is complicated and in part became dependent upon the effect of Itkin's personality. As is made clear in contributions by other writers, Itkin created and dissolved and created again (and dissolved again), thrusting his restless energy into whatever field of activity which interested him. He was not alone in this behavior, although he may have been extreme. We all were involved in fits and starts. In the prairie city in which I went to college, we at different times tried a gay coffee house, a coffee house for former patients at the local mental hospital, advocacy for the mentally ill, an alternative 'zine, and more; all short-lived. (The one project which did endure was the "head shop." It provided helpful paraphernalia for the home and also made money.) So, it was not solely Itkin's personal strengths and failings that mattered. He was of the times.

His importance lies in that he dealt with matters outside of temporal concern. He dealt with the spirit and community of the spirit and the place of gay people therein.

In further considering Itkin's call for community in *The Radical Jesus,* his critique and approaches are thoroughly relevant today. His language is dated only in that it responded to the circumstances before him, and in that its urgency was rarely accompanied by equivalent activity. We, however, are still afforded an opportunity to use his thinking in addressing the spiritual milieu of our own time. Itkin writes:

> In our day, the church bearing Jesus' name has few prophetic voices to sound above the noise of violence and destruction, of sexism and violence. Perhaps this is in large part because the church has lost the Spirit which empowered it with strength for struggle with the leviathan forces of the state before Nicea: not entirely lost, however, for there have always been those who resisted both the violence of the state and the oppressiveness of the institutional church to stand fast in the Good News of Jesus and to transform the world through his revolutionary love.

He then goes on to quote George MacLeod, "I simply argue that the Cross be raised again at the center of the market place as well as on the steeple of a church."

The capitulation of Christianity to the command of the mercantile state has since at least the fourth century been the great curse upon the people. All of subsequent history's horrible events and effects are in some measure attributable to this union. Mainstream Christian Churches make no attempt to disguise their fondness for the dollar. From Reverend Ike and Joel Osteen proclaiming that wealth is the sure sign of God's love, to the Rector of St. Thomas Fifth Avenue rejoicing at the nearly one and one-half million received in pledges in 2007, it is central to the worship. Or, it is the worship? What is god's name? It is therefore necessary to locate any discussion of community and living spirituality in the lap of this marriage of the diabolical.

There was, correspondingly, a genuine revolution in the USA in the 1960s and '70s. It is one that in a sense flew under the radar, except for those who knew. It was this: In every major university, departments of economics were transformed into schools of business administration, producing in thousands the robed robbers of the MBA. For the first time, a critical mass of educated, bright, young people, imbued in the ideological correctness of greed, burst upon a society and without a moment of self doubt began to remake it in their own image. This was greed and profit, not just for its own sake, as the reason for living. Is it a religion now? It is more than that. It is the all. It means that every aspect of human activity is being restructured, privatized, as they call it, in a way such that it will yield a profit. So clever and thorough is the planning involved that now major catastrophes open opportunities for a profitable remaking of entire parts of the globe. This is currently occurring New Orleans. After the events of 9–11, the advice of President Bush to the people was to "pray and go shopping."

Anyone can identify the ever-deepening intrusion of capitalism into the workings of daily life. This intrusion goes beyond simply controlling how one spends one's money. It is a struggle for the souls of humanity. Is there a resistance to it? Resistance from mainstream religion takes the form of the lie which it has always used: pie in the sky, in the bye and bye (until then accept your lot). If this is not sufficient, capital provides more satisfactory alternatives: alcohol and drug usage, sports, shopping and other Disney-worlds.

It is difficult to pinpoint (although not that difficult!) the parties responsible, for, as Itkin describes in 1972, "This kind of collective evil is of the sort that no individual is really responsible for. It s caused by that faceless and omnipresent "they" who are at the same time both everything and no one in particular." The point here is that it is our voluntary participation in the movement of capitalism that makes this penultimate take-over of the human soul so successful and so difficult to combat. Nevertheless, if not countered, extracting the soul from its capitalist incarnation may become impossible:

> This is the power of the demonic which, while originating in collective human will, is a power over which human will has lost control and to which humanity at large has fallen casualty. Even those who are obviously its beneficiaries are as much its slaves and victims as those who are its chief targets.

Such a statement comes from a sanguine and forgiving view of human kind, essential to the work of fixing and healing, and perhaps creating a spiritual community in the midst of life.

The work is making manifest the love of Jesus, in which Itkin has great confidence:

> In the old terms, then, Jesus comes as an exorcist: one of the basic signs of His Presence is the act of breaking the power of the "demonic" over human life.... True exorcism is the activity of total humanity present in the person, the activity of Love. It is the activity of personhood beyond ego, where life is without competitiveness or lordship. This is where Jesus is present as we are, that we may be as He is, and we may experience wholeness, both of one's own being and of that integrated with the whole of life. As St. Clement of Alexandria says, "The Word of God became man, so that you might learn from man how man becomes God."

And the call that Itkin makes *to act* is clear:

> In order to fulfill our responsibilities, we must awaken the divine potential within; for ourselves, for those in the communities we live and work with, for brothers and sisters we have never seen, and for generations yet unborn.

Itkin was moving into an understanding of the true self, the indwelling Christ, and the need to bring it forth. In manifesting love from just such a source as the genuine self which lies within every person, things then become truly possible.

This "Love" is the basis for his gay Christian church and his community which are one in the same. By gay, Itkin meant homosexual people, but not these alone,

> but rather a lifestyle in which love, trust, and support between all people supplant relationships based on hate, fear and competitive aggression. Gay is a process of attaining mutual and equal social and sensual relationships among all human beings.

But, gays were to play a leading role in the new Ecclesia, based in their undenied history of oppression. More is expected of them: "...gay people, together with all people seeking liberation, are called to prepare a people that shall be fit for the Liberator."

It is not a bad fit. Expecting that gay people are just the ones to grasp and put into action the reasonable ideal of creating a loving community has precedents. We do this. In the early days of the epidemic, we came out of the woodwork to take care of our own sick and dying. It was to be seen to be believed. Or, how many of us, by desire, or forced by circumstances of an unloving blood family have made for ourselves a family of friends? It is the friends we love most, often more than lovers. In the current climate of marriage urgency, is it not often a friend we marry? (Marriage? — Itkin may have screamed at this trend. We do not need to be "better" heterosexual couples, or better anything which replicates the hetero-capitalist command.) But, as they say, "not for nothing," would gays today re-evaluate their view of the world and their independence. It would be the major challenge for an Itkin-church to get the attention of and breach the wall of resistance with today's gays. Yet add a couple of necessary ingredients; these families of friends can become the nesting place of a new Ecclesia.

In describing the Ecclesia as community, Itkin wrote:

> Such a radical gay Christian Church must seek to apply the insights of the apostolic and primitive Church-Community if Jesus to he needs if contemporary gay people: offering the Bread of Life to those who never before have been offered anything but the stones of rejection, neglect and oppression. In the turmoil of this oppression, in the face of this rejection and neglect, in the center of the cyclone that is our struggle for freedom, we hear the Call of the Bible: "You are a people holy to the Lord your God, and the Lord has chosen you out of all peoples on earth to be His special people" (Deut. 14:2). "We are no more strangers and foreigners, but fellow-citizens with the saints and of the household of God...."
>
> The alternative, the only effective ministry now, the only ministry which can truly reach alienated people, is a community of serving people, following in the foot steps, the sometimes bloody footsteps, of Jesus as the person for others and sharing in the life-styles of those being served....
>
> The Way of Life in Jesus has two functions: external and internal. The external is the outward reach in love and service, in relationship, in the sharing and expression of Jesus' Love in action, towards all humanity

> and all of the cosmos… In its internal function this takes the form of work on oneself, the search within one's own depths for union with Jesus, with the life Divine.
>
> Each of us must undertake the long and difficult — and joyous — process of living the life: as we have worshipped Jesus in prayer and sacrament, now we must go out and seek him in every face.

In our time, stressing the internal, personal aspect of a spiritual life may be the best hope of success. Many, many people seem genuinely concerned about this. The trick, then, becomes to locate personal spirit within the spirit of the whole, expose alienation and defeat separatism.

One might criticize, saying that Itkin is light on details of what his Ecclesia would actually do. His intent here is working on attitudes and setting parameters. This is the struggle for the attention of the reader or hearer. If one gets some people involved and active then the detail questions will come up. It may have been his strength to work on this level and leave the details to others. His words were and are clearly stirring. For him the Spirit is still moving over the waters.

> In this alternative community we must come to the place where it seems that the fellowship is filled with rush of a mighty wind and tongue of fire over every head, and suddenly we are wedded into one. Then we can go out from the Community with the power of the spirit of Jesus and change the world. When sometimes it seems hard and you feel that many demands are being made upon you, think of our gay brothers and sisters out in the streets, and how much they need what we are putting together in such a Community. If we don't put it together, nobody else will, and our sisters and brothers are going to be destroyed.

> And if they are destroyed, we will be destroyed
> with them, and perhaps by them.

This is a vision of biblical proportions and, depending upon your viewpoint, prescient.

Thus Itkin presented his dream of the Ecclesia-Community, the "army of lovers" with a dose of healthy Christian *mores*, a clear view of the role of service and a stinging critique of capital. A beautiful dream, and a genuine starting place.

If presented today to unsuspecting gays, of whatever type, would it be received seriously? This is the question everyone keeps coming back to. So much has happened since Itkin published *The Radical Jesus*. Oppression and rejection have not subsided, but alongside of that, gays have made huge gains in society. We have learned to co-exist with hatred, sometimes walking past it, sometimes yelling back at it, sometimes withholding our rather considerable wealth.

Then there is the epidemic, a horror beyond comprehension which, like the Great War, took away a generation or more of, chiefly, our brothers. It is still with us, yea, even here in the USA.

There is the growth of a newly empowered source of danger. The religious Right posses a threat to life. It is a force capable of anything, including murder. If fascism comes to America, it will come on the wings of a snow white dove.

That aside, given daily life, is there a need for the kind of community envisioned by Itkin? There is no question that there is. If for no other reason, it is necessary to have a countervailing force to the exponentially increasing control by capital. As mentioned, every act involved in living is or soon will be mediated by a profit-making relationship. It is ironic that capitalism may actually be defeated, not by human endeavor, but by nature, which can no longer tolerate the assault. Of course, that final conflict is a long way off in years, and its result will not be good for humanity.

An Itkin community today would:

— face as intense a struggle for hearts and minds as it ever did;
— of necessity form a strong core of worker-saints who, firm in the conviction of the Love of Jesus, would carry out direct service to people;
— different segments of the gay community require differing actions;
— the well-heeled, of which there are many, now face loss of soul by their dedication to the dictates of the capitalistic ruling class;
— communities of color suffer acutely from racism and classism, and also, their youth are being infected with HIV in frightening numbers;
— for all segments, especially again among color and the poor, it is as if being gay is itself the death sentence; getting infected is merely fulfilling one's role in the Thantocracy;
— work to protect our gains, for they are still fragile, and strive for more;
— reconsider the role of promiscuous sex — it is our nature, whether we act on it or speculate on it, the Ecclesia community could develop the idea and practice of sacral sex, in which sexual patterns of all types are given the extra dimension and responsibility of being acts of divinity and as such are carried out as if each one were a vital, significant moment in the life of each participant (which is the case, anyway). (Do I hear snickers? This would be tough, and also, it is difficult to compete with the extraordinary sense of ecstasy gotten from sex + meth and/or cocaine);
— confront gay particularism, rumor-mongering and gossip, not small issues;
— create actual programs, for example, every city might want to have a group home for older gays, facing isolation;
— explore and foster our natural shamanistic abilities.

All of living, of course, becomes the concern of the Itkin Ecclesia-Community, in direct competition with capitalist society's assault upon the same.

+Don Stouder, in writing about Itkin, quoted from his journal:

> The Christ himself, our Lord Jesus Christ, appeared to me, both suffering and glorified, and told me he has saved the whole of creation, even me. It is enough. God has blessed me and I should be satisfied.

"I should be satisfied"? Maybe he is not satisfied. Maybe, because he could stand on the threshold of true goodness, he could see that it is indeed possible. Let us also not be satisfied, unless like our dear +Mikhail Itkin, we tear at the power of the archons and set in motion the other way.

26 June 2008
Oratory of S. Pelagius
Jersey City, New Jersey

About the Contributors

Michael Elliot Bacon, born and raised on the prairie, a graduate of the University of Nebraska, has lived and worked on the margins of society. He was and is active in certain causes and in spiritual exploration. On May 6, 2006 (Mikhail Itkin Day), he was made an Independent Catholic priest by one of the editors of this book (Mark Aelred). He is currently working to translate inspired text from the Gospels of Philip and Thomas into liturgical forms.

Gary Roscoe Johnson, a second-generation tattooist/body-piercer at Johnson Tattoo, is carrying on a Detroit-area legacy started by his father in 1965. He is a graphic designer, anarcho-surrealist, veteran of the pre-internet 'zine revolution, hoarder, follower of Jesus, and curator of the Poopenheimer Archives. He proudly bears the word "NO" tattooed on his tongue in 3CM-tall block letters.

Rosamonde Miller is a mystic, spiritual teacher, and the founder of the Gnostic Sanctuary (Ecclesia Gnostica Mysteriorum) in the San Francisco Bay area. She is an ordained priest and a consecrated bishop in two Gnostic traditions and contributor to several books such as *The Allure of Gnosticism, Strange Vocation: Independent Bishops Tell Their Stories* and *Mary of Magdala: A Gnostic Fable.* She has coined the term "wild gnosis" to describe her mystical approach, and "urban mystic," to speak of the ability to fully live in the spirit while being at ease in the midst of city life and chaos.

John P. Plummer studied theology at Fordham University, Vanderbilt University, and the Graduate Theological Foundation. He has been involved with independent sacramental churches for almost thirty years, and is the author of a number of books and articles on the subject, most notably *The Many Paths of the Independent Sacramental Movement* and *Living Mysteries.* He lives in Nashville, Tennessee, and welcomes contact by email (john.plummer@comcast.net) or twitter (@priestcraft).

Mark Aelred Sullivan, a life-long student of spiritual and social philosophies, published *The Storm! A Journal for Free Spirits* (1976–87), and edited the Post-Centenary edition of John Henry Mackay's *The Anarchists: A Picture of Civilization at the Close of the Nineteenth Century* (1999, Autonomedia). In 1992, he founded a universal Gnostic ministry, Circle of the Free Spirit, becoming its bishop, Aelred, in 1995. Mark is active with the American Buddhist Study Center. Through Earth-Sharing Associates and Insight Out, Inc., Mark participates with his partner, Osamu Uehara, in performing arts productions that promote a fair society.

Ian Young, born in London in 1945, was involved in the early Gay Liberation movement in Toronto, London and New York City. He has been a poet, essayist, columnist, editor, publisher, bibliographer and short-story writer. His books include *Sex Magick, The Male Muse, The Stonewall Experiment, Out in Paperback* and *Encounters with Authors.* His work has appeared in many anthologies, including *The Mammoth Book of Gay Short Stories, The Golden Age of Gay Fiction, What Love Is* and *Bizarre Dreams.* He is the proprietor of Sykes Press, a Toronto publishing house specializing in memoirs.